# TERRIAN JOURNALS'

# IWITFULNESS

(The incomplete works of
unabridged and unrestrained laughter.)

I0149654

(disc jockey)
**by Donald Murray Anderson**

**Iwitfulness**
**A Mythbreaker Book**
**First Edition**
© **Copyright 2023 by Donald Murray Anderson**

ISBN 978-1-989593-38-7

All rights reserved. Without limiting rights under copyright reserved above, no part of this book may be reproduced, stored in or introduced into a retrieval system, or transmitted in any form or by any means (electronic, mechanical, photocopying, recording, or otherwise) without prior written permission of the copyright owner.

For information address: mythbreaker@mail.com

Dear Reader,

Prepare for a voyage of crisscrossing and obliterating the not so fine line between genius and insanity. The humour in this volume is definitely crazy.

Always know that my humour truly goes viral. If I get it, you get it, whether you like it or not.

As part of one churchist zombie chant puts it, this humour is "beyond all understanding".

It goes from incomprehensible enigmas to knee-slapping silly, extrapolating from a lifetime of unbridled and unchecked spelling and grammatical errors.

Buckle up and over in thoughtful and spasmodic involuntary laughter.

Signed,

The Author of this affront to reason and sanity

In this piece of work, "What's so funny" is both a question and an answer.

## Dedication: To the humourless

In serious, humble, and submissive recognition of the humourless bureaucracy and "security" enforcers surrounding us and abusing us, this volume acknowledges their shockingly nonchalant and automatically accepted contributions to teaching us all how to passively submit, with straight faces without smile creases, and with internally and eternally bleeding lips from biting them to hold back mocking expressions and pathetic laughter at jokes we dare not say out loud in the presence of the humourless.

Security forbids the freedom of speech called joking.

Uttering humourous thoughts is a crime that is punishable by arbitrary detainment and indefinite detention for questioning and personal life investigation.

This autocratic monarchical-like "security" dictatorship does not tolerate court jesters or comic relief in any form.

To joke about "security" is at your own risk.

The figurehead monarchs of España and Thailand truly are amused by all the newer "security" laws against the supremely disrespectful insult called humour.

Such reckless behaviour in the presence of absolute security only invites harsh ridicule, i.e. very unpleasant humour, along with constant surveillance and relentless persecution. "You're asking for it!"

This unquestionable and unchallengeable security diety blocking our every smile and path each time that we venture out or even attempt to move, is training us to be submissive and silent.

Security is training us how to: raise our arms; turn around like a toy top; undergo not so magic "wanding"; submit to "random 'enhanced" procedures; accept messy and ineffective rifling through our neatly-packed belongings, including our most intimate underwear, (with unsterilized dirty plastic gloves which only protect the wearer and contribute to the transmission of bacterial infections, illness, fatal viruses and to the onset of pandemics); accept mandatory physical assault searches as "normal", etc.

For being "good boy!" or "good girl!" during security training, security will let us stand on our hind legs and catch a little treat.

The little treat is the right to passage.

Of course we must roll over, beg, play dead, forget all about human rights and personal freedoms, and abandon democracy altogether, "for security reasons".

The present volume of inquisitive, critical, and unblushingly silly humour is also dedicated to my very serious and humourless elementary school teachers who, unable to cope with a smiling, happy pupil, always shouted, "Wipe that smirk off your face!"

Before, after, and beyond school hours, I'm still having a happy childhood. I learn so much more when school is out.

When I'm finally out of the schooling system for good, I'm beaming with delight at university campuses.

At last I'm free to learn and express myself after 12 years of schooling oppression.   But the psychic trauma of elementary school is very challenging to overcome.

Elementary school teachers who routinely demand docile submission by telling pupils to "Sit down and shut up!" are not providing the best preparation for asking questions in lectures or public meetings, participating in seminar groups or opinion polls, or talking an employer into giving a raise.

No wonder more recent generations of pupils are becoming more rambunctious and rebellious in some classrooms. They are their forebears' messengers*.

(*In some cases, ex-pupils turned "helicopter parents" lead the rebellion assault, conducting a continuous pre-emptive strike to wipe out all childhood thinking and self-confidence.  I call them caretaker society parents.)

The impact of the initial assault of the humourless school teachers on me is evident in my grade one elementary school class photograph.

I look like a traumatized juvenile offender convict at a high security correctional institution.   As my dad often says, "Never laugh at a dictator."

Fortunately, I never lose the "smirk" that everyone else recognizes as a shy and friendly smile.  It gets me more compliments than anything else about my appearance.

At least I get the last laughs too, with a very happy life.

**No kidding
to get your goat?**

This volume of humour goes far beyond kidding around, entering the realm of "What am I saying?!" and "Why am I laughing?!"

Sometimes we laugh because something is funny. Sometimes we laugh to be polite. Sometimes we laugh because everyone around us is laughing.

And sometimes we laugh because we don't know any better.

You are now crossing the slim boundary between comedy and pathos. Can you tell? Please do.

### Final report?

"I'm finding a lot of things funny lately, and I'm not sure they are."

-Lieutenant First Class Ellen Louise Ripley, last survivor of the Nostromo Lockmart CM-88B Bison M-Class star freighter after encounter with Xenomorph XX121.

Welcome to Iwitfulness:
Where funny meets strange.

## Unremovable humour

Something funny is going on here. That means a joke is not coming off? You're putting me on, right?

# Before and about face

## Why a third?

Why am I writing my third book of humour? I have no idea. Why not?

Okay, I'll make something up to explain it. Let me delve into creative writing. Here goes something:

I'm writing a third because a quarter is too small and a half is too big. Seriously, folks, I'm writing the third book because my first two turned out sort of funny.

I can't help it. It's out of my control and my mind.

I won't call <u>Iwitfulness</u> "the hat trick" because that's originally a cricket term. I don't mean the insect, just the less interesting "game".

Cricket is baseball without all the suspense, action, and excitement.

Cricket is spread around the world by the U.K.'s empire.

The "game" gives local people something to do with wickets other than standing in line in front of them waiting for service from the U.K. occupation "colonial office" bureaucracy.

Cricket also provides locals with a non-violent alternative to using bats for thrashing the "colonial office" bureaucrats and sending them packing.

I keep my distance from cricket bats. They might carry viruses.

But I'm no stranger to curling, even though my hair is naturally so.

I have some experience with sliding back and forth on a strip of ice with a rock and broom, if only a few times during two winters. Thus, I hit rock bottom.

The experience makes me wonder about curling irons. It seems very strange to iron something to make it anything other than flat and straight. Besides an iron melts ice.

Or are curling irons specially-designed golf clubs that the manufacturers guarantee will always result in slicing and hooking shots?

I mean the ones on the fairway, not at the 19th hole or in desperation due to gender abuse and discrimination.

All in all, I prefer golf to curling for the same reason that I prefer baseball. One person shouting "Sweep!" doesn't thrill me like "Easy out!" and "Heavy hitter!"

Golf gives me the excitement of driving poorly without being inebriated, without a license, and with no concern about being arrested or becoming involved in an accident.

Golf also enables me to add elements of suspense and mystery to my golfing.

I wonder which way the ball is going to go and where it will land. Then I have to wonder where it does land. I'm blindsided?

I only hope it's on a green rather than in the rough or in a sand trap. I often never know.

My late friend and golf partner Takeshi says that I put so many balls into the trees that he expects to find golf ball trees growing wherever I play.

You'd think that my proclivity toward landing in trees would result in me getting at least one birdie or perhaps an eagle. But I even avoid fowl language.

Golf leaves me perplexed.

Since everywhere on a golf course is green, how can anyone find "a" green? When I finally do find one, I actually can exhibit some skill and power.

It's like playing perpendicular billiards on an uneven table.

As for rough, it's where my golf game too often remains. I also tend to get trapped in sand as if it were a bunker sheltering me from a better score.

I hit the golf ball so many times that I lose count. Perhaps I should use multiples of ten, as in $10^{12}$.

Okay, I'm just being funny. But isn't that the whole point?

Now where was I? Oh yes, writing something about the third book of humour. And here it comes now. But I can only shout, "Three!", not "Four!", so far.

This attempt at humour is bound to provoke a belly laugh in even the mildly-amused, somewhat obese person.

## It's all a blurb

What's so funny!?  Isn't <u>TJ JNG</u> supposed to be "the first and last of a series, maybe"?  Maybe indeed!

Then comes <u>Half Serious (and wit)</u>.  Now there's a new word title, <u>Iwitfulness</u>.

This one goes further yet beyond the serious world, boldly going so far as to attempt to dissect, understand, and analyze humour and laughter itself.

Can there ever be a fourth volume after this one?  Funny you should ask.  Is that the next title?  Will there ever truly be a last laugh?  You must be joking!

These books should not and cannot be taken seriously. Having hysterical conniptions and dying laughing, only then would the author be dead serious.

<u>Terrian Journals</u>' humour books are writing from an age when "dumb down" is often heard, but "Smarten up!" almost vanishes from daily parlance.

This writing comes from a time when people with children talk critically and seriously about not burdening their descendants with debt, while refusing to bequeath their children a planet compatible with human life.

It's a moment when the elite and worried passively and ritually attend serious "Save Earth!" rallies and conferences, arriving in a cavalcade of polluting air and surface vehicles.

It's an era when some politicians and weird optimists celebrate melting polar ice caps for providing access to more of the same fossil fuels causing the ice to melt and reducing the likelihood of the continued existence of the human species.

It's an epoch when billionaire oligarchs build underground bunkers so that they can look forward to enjoying being the last people alive on a planet that's no longer capable of supporting human life.

Billionaire oligarchs don't consider themselves human?

How demeaning that would be!

Hedging their bets on solitude and isolation, billionaire oligarchs also send themselves into outer space, so that they can corner the real estate market on already uninhabitable planets.

Yes, the humour in <u>Terrian Journals</u>' humour books originates when comedy, pathos, and tragedy not only meet, they get so tightly intertwined that they become indistinguishable.

At this very moment, ignorance goes so far beyond bliss that it reaches euphoric nihilism.

In contemporary news, the former broadcasting lineups break up into chaotic headlines and disjointed contradictory tales.

It might be funny if it weren't true. But it's no laughing matter.

Climate change warnings are mixed up with complaints about gasoline price increases, holidays filling roads with polluting vehicles, and wider road demands to reduce traffic congestion.

New labels on alcohol drug containers warning that this product causes cancer, etc. are interspersed with complaints about raising taxes on alcohol and the laments of bar owners.

Much the same happens when nicotine is the most popular drug of choice.

Illness, death, and health department law suits against nicotine cartels silence complaints.
While attempting to consume this smorgasbord of mixed up messages, news audiences are served an indigestible menu of commentary.

Minds are swayed by speculative "analysts", "specialists", "experts", and ill-informed "influencers", i.e. the new fortune tellers and soothsayers who talk continuously and endlessly make comments about unknown facts and hypothetical questions beyond their knowledge.

As <u>Alice In Wonderland</u> puts it, "They fill my mind with ideas, but I don't know what they are."

The former news broadcasting lineups are now a hodgepodge of flash mob reporting split from all else, leaving us not laughing but whimpering.

The "style books" are tossed into the garbage, or burned, and the tough editors all retire and now live in total off-the-grid seclusion, having no remote sensors or contact with what's now news.

The last laugh becomes a joke at the expense of all of us. We are all the expendable butts of humour.

No-brainer cyberspace airhead videos spread faster than Ebola and Bubonic plague, until death do us part our crossed eyes*, dulled minds, and blank stares at screens, as we blink toward total obliviousness and oblivion. (*Crossed eyes are formerly used in comic strips to indicate that a character is dead. It's a religionist thing?)

Satirical, thoughtful, critical, and deceptively or truly silly humour are all to be bureaucratically re-categorized, redefined, regulated, and relegated to the least or seldom read corner of page 2, or to token non-journalistic comments in letters to the editor, in a newspaper with declining readership due to a fatal case of pandemic attention span deficiency.

No worries, it will all be censored, er, I mean "redacted", and not rédacter by a rédacteur (français) who is attempting to keep us all fully informed.

The only remaining placement giving refuge to such "cerebral" humour is to get it declared suitable only for the most obscure locations in the unnumbered pages of <u>Terrian Journals' Jokes Nobody Gets</u> and subsequent volumes of humour which might appear in this seriously and totally funny series.

### Forgotten joke

Completing <u>Terrian Journals Half Serious (and wit)</u>, I inadvertently forget to include a joke.  So here it is, for another humour volume?

The spice Rosemary is supposed to be good for one thing. I don't remember what.

# Laughing matter:
## taking humour seriously

Serious, very serious, and overly-serious people often sternly say or shout, "This is no laughing matter!".

It's an expression that can be misused in a defensive manner to block, avoid, and lose an opportunity for debate and dissent.

It prevents people from introducing a different perspective, or offering some comic relief.

When a verbal humour blockade is imposed, perhaps only court jesters under monarchical dictatorship don't fear losing their heads when they mirthfully and unwittingly lose them.

Jesters might feel safe that they won't lose their heads unless their "divine lords" lose theirs, or their sense of humour, or unless the inbred elite "lords" actually possess the intelligence to understand the mocking banter of the jesters all too well.

Laughing at a dictator can be perilous and fatal. But laughing at a dictator is irresistible, unavoidable, inevitable, involuntary, and essential.

It's delightful and such a great release from the tension, stress, tragedy, and horror of dictatorship.

At heart, laughing at a dictator is no different from any other laughter. except for the death-defying risk aspect.

Although laughter at the dictators in schooling, policing, religionisms, and employment may not seem quite so risky, the consequences can be lifelong, and potentially life-ending, in at least the sense of losing the ability to have a fulfilling life. Dictators disable people.

All authoritarian figures can do you in, one way or another. But that's not unique.

Apparently, insulting a "head of state" is still forbidden and punishable by law in many "democratic" nation-states, including ones on the European peninsula of Asia.

In more general terms, prejudice and discrimination against the humorous are real and have decisive consequences, not the least of which is, ironically, not to be taken seriously in any endeavour.

"S/he's not a serious person and shouldn't be taken seriously." is a way of cursing a person to irrelevance and insignificance. People who aren't serious are to be ignored.

Terms such as "You're joking!", "You can't be serious!", "Don't be silly.", "Get serious.", and even "Seriously!" are at least admonitions cautioning the humorists not to pursue their mocking and jibing directed at the serious of the world.

Seriously humourless people will pounce and strike serious blows against anyone finding them funny, instead of taking them dead seriously and depicting them as such.

Dead serious is a very appropriate and accurate description of those who discourage and punish humour. They are brain dead?

In some nation-states, making jokes about the powerfully serious people, serious edicts of religionisms, and other absolutely serious things can result in arrest, conviction, and imprisonment, if not execution.

As mentioned earlier, those who ridicule some of the easiest targets, such as the symbolically anachronistic titular monarchs in España and Thailand, do so at their peril, while comedians in the U.K. regularly make fun of their monarchs in often biting satire.

Yet the reactions to humour directed at monarchy in the realms of España and Thailand are at least strangely and ironically funny, particularly in España's case.

España's Generalissimo F. Franco fights in a civil war against a monarchy and becomes the only openly F. for Fascist dictator left in power thirty years after Deutschland's Fuhrer and Italia's El Duce are defeated militarily and long dead.

F. Franco remains in power, a forgotten relic Fascist dictator for a total of about 40 years.

The Allied Forces and United Nations don't notice him, or one Fascist regime is okay?

By the time that Franco's regime ends, his realm is one of many Fascist regimes around the world, particularly in the southern Americas.

There, murderous Fascist regimes are all staunch and seriously bloodthirsty allies of "the west" in the "Cold War", i.e. the U.S.A. versus the C.C.C.P.

Franco is a model Fascist for all allies of "the west" to follow, and for all "communist" dictatorships too.

Apparently, by the time F. Franco dies of old age while still in office, he doesn't remember how he gets there. His legacy is quite bizarre.

He bequeaths España to the very monarchy that he defeats in civil war and he founds a democratic system. He expects the restored monarch to be Franco II?

After España's long, bloody civil war, followed by about 40 years of brutal and murderous dictatorship, during which every pro-democracy movement is quashed and España's regions are driven to separatism by Franco, he sees no contradiction in restoring all that he opposes since the beginning of his era.

So Franco is perpetrating a preposterous running joke against the monarchy of España, the pro-democracy advocates, and even his lifelong supporters.

Just kidding about the Fascism?

For this blood-stained "humour", España's monarchy does not immediately and unceremoniously dump F. Franco's dead corpse into a pit in the yard of a Spanish prison.

The bigger the joke, the fewer the consequences?

Thailand's monarchy is also ridiculed by a military dictatorship.

The generals use the reigning monarch as a symbolic puppet in a Punch and Judy show vs. pro-democracy supporters.

Under this military dictatorship, the only "legal" laughter possible would come from the generals in power if the monarch were to say, openly and seriously, that he wanted the generals to prepare for a fully democratically-elected government.

The military dictatorship already mocks and precludes the advent of such a government by stationing military personnel in one third of the seats of Thailand's parliament, just like Burma/Mynmar's military dictatorship.

Instead of enabling voters to fill these seats in free and fair elections, the military dictatorship posts its seat guards and orders them how to vote.

They can thus plea that they are "just following order" every time that they do the military dictatorship's bidding.

If anyone should tell them, with a straight face, that they cannot make fun of the monarch, they might subtly smirk faintly at the idea, or they might "bust a gut" laughing.

The monarch has no say in anything.

The generals are remaining in charge of everything in Thailand, and by so doing they are exposing Thailand's monarchy as a meaningless joke.

It's too subtle to be punished? No, military dictators are above the law that they impose. And that's not a very high hurdle to almost effortlessly step over.

Non-monarchical religionisms also impose serious consequences for forbidden humour. Thus the expression: "He laughed. He almost died."

In fact, a humorous "wrongdoer" can almost literally die laughing.

Even authors and editorial cartoonists do not always enjoy universal freedom of expression, whether sincere, hypocritical, or cynical.

People working at publications in Norge and France are murdered for their humour.

They aggressively make fun of a particular religionism and its founder and claim that they have the right to do so because they have legally guaranteed freedom of expression.

But they're hypocritically biased and extremely prejudiced. The don't even try to play fair by also lampooning their own supernatural religionism and its founder the same way.

They don't publish a cartoon image of Jesus laughing while believers in Judaism are lead to their deaths in Nazi gas chambers.

Why? Because it sounds and is grotesque. It is a "sick joke" when extended to the "humorists'" own religionism.

So why accuse people adhering to other religionisms of "lacking a sense of humour" when their religionisms are attacked in like manner?

If it's not a laughing matter for you, why should it be taken as a joke by someone not sharing your perspective?

Why not follow your own religionism's teachings that tell you to "do unto others..."?

Since the cartoonist jokers in Norge and France probably know that quotation, why are they mocking other people's religionism and maliciously attacking its founder?

It smacks of the superiority complex of the 500 year European national-colonial era. The enduring legacy of that era is that non-Europeans can never be taken seriously?

The non-European world is forever an inferior joke?

## Choice targets

What is so different from mocking others' religionisms and their founders and mocking people because they have different physiological sexual characteristics and orientations or skin pigmentation and eye-lid angles?

When I ask this question to people who mockingly torment others for not using non-medical drugs such as alcohol, some tell me that ridiculing abstainers is fair because the abstainers are not born abstainers.

This makes abstainers quite different from females, blacks, and orientals. They don't have an easy escape route. They would have to become trans-racial and trans-sexual?

I'm hearing: They are forever stuck with their inferior non-male, non-European birth identities?!

In great contrast, the argument goes, abstainers can stop being abstainers.

In this easy way they can change their behaviour to escape critical ridicule. They are making a choice by not changing.

If they stubbornly refuse to change, they must be prepared to always be constantly, regularly, and routinely challenged, criticized, and mocked for being different. It's normal!

They can make their lives easier by simply conforming with "majority" behaviour.

Sounds like the motto over the front door of a Canadian residential school, a "nice" concentration camp for First Nations children.

All "non-conforming" people who are simply expressing their freedom of choice are fair game for ridicule or questioning?

Their only escape is to demonstrate absolute conformity with the domineering, dominating social behaviour?

So, logically, it's all right to mock all people who exercise their freedom of choice? Freedom of choice is a joke?

I obviously disagree.

Humour isn't merely a weapon for attacking everyone except oneself or for attacking "non-conforming" choices.

Humour is about give and take. If you can't take it don't give it.

### European values

Although the prices and bank charges are a shock here, I have to commend Belgium (and neighbouring Luxembourg) for not charging admission to museums.

But I wonder if this means that museums are the least important places in the European peninsula.

I find much smaller places which do charge admission fees.

These places must be the most precious ones in European societies. Otherwise, why pay for them but not the museums?

These European admission-charging places are called toilets.

## Alien invaders

So many corners of western Asia's Eur are being invaded by the diabolical, garbage-pail-from-outer-space, super-pay toilets which I first sight in Paris, a year and a half earlier.

This space débris is spreading over the European Community like dog feces.

Every time I see one I feel like urinating on the wall or defecating on these tombs commemorating the death of natural, free behaviour.

Yet while human urine and feces on city sidewalks is indecent and illegal, similar behaviour from dogs is quite all right, free of charge, and an unpopular tourist sight everywhere.

## Involuntary hysteria

During my first four years in Toronto, an acquaintance invites me to her apartment for supper. This is our first and last meal together.

I don't qualify for another invitation and I don't reciprocate by inviting her to eat because I'm not interested in her personally or in what she might decide to offer me.

She prepares a truly delicious meal for our supper and I thoroughly enjoy the evening with the exception of one unpleasant moment.

That's when she asks me about one of my personal lifestyle choices by saying, "Isn't that peculiar?"

If this question were posed in a joking tone, or followed by a friendly laugh, it might be all right.

But she asks the question in a deadly serious tone, as if I am doing something fundamentally wrong in my life and must explain myself or face social ostracism and ridicule.

I'm completely and profoundly surprised by the apparent personal attack coming from a person with whom I share no history or animosity.

I'm particularly surprised because she belongs to a group of people who have the self-image of progressive and open-minded supporters of fairness and freedom of choice.

Yet she's not surprised with herself and doesn't pause and reflect upon why she asks me the question.

Fortunately, her question turns out to be an unintentional cruel insult and not an aggressive attempt to depict my personal choices in life as an indication that I don't have the adult right to choose for myself.

When I mention this incident to a mutual friend, she tells me that my host is overflowing with serious and sincere apologies for being offensive.

At least that's what our mutual friend says. I never hear anything about it directly from my host.

But the unfortunate incident is only one bad moment in what is for me a very pleasant, long, and mirthful evening going well beyond my expectations.

I'm invited to supper for two specific purposes. I'm here at her apartment tonight, socializing with her for the first time because she's looking for either two people or one.

One is a co-renter. She's looking for someone to occupy her apartment's second bedroom and so decrease her monthly living costs.

She's a cooperative housing activist who lives in a privately-owned apartment building. I don't know why and don't ask if it's peculiar for a coop supporter not to live in a coop.

At the same time, she recently disposes of a long-term boyfriend and is consequently now looking for someone to replace him.

The search for a replacement boyfriend is her current project when I arrive for supper.

She places a personal ad in the classified section of a daily newspaper to recruit a new boyfriend.

This is long before on-line dancing around other people to find a mate, and falling in love with cyberspace virtual dating websites.

In the ancient newspaper ad age of my acquaintance, a personal ad results in a pile of paper replies sent to the advertiser for review, via a newspaper postal box.

She shows me her pile. Quite a number of men send her their photographs along with typed and signature-bearing self-descriptions.

They're like résumés submitted to a potential employer.

This is all serious and we don't joke about it.

She tells me which candidates for her position seem more attractive than others. It's not merely about their appearances in the pictures.

She asks me to read the résumés and to comment if I wish to do so. I don't really have any say in the matter or anything to say.

Instead, early on, I find myself having a spontaneous, unrestrainable, uncontrollable laughing fit. I'm not consciously laughing at the advertising campaign or the replies.

I don't know why I'm laughing so much. I have no conscious reason that I can perceive. I'm not overly tired or stressed. I'm quite relaxed and feeling good.

My host seems as puzzled as I am by my unexpected laughing fit. Neither one of us can figure it out. I apologize for it, but she doesn't seem to be offended.

Perhaps I laugh myself out of getting onto the short list for both the co-renter and the new boyfriend positions.

After listening to me laugh for quite a while, we part amicably at the door as I thank her for the good meal and enjoyable evening.

I have no idea why it's enjoyable. But it is unique.

This story is my way of introducing some reflections on laughter itself. I'm considering what I know about it.

### Lots of laughs, out loud and not

I think there is authentic laughter, as I experience it that evening in Toronto, and feigned laughter, which I hear everywhere else.

Feigned laughter can be out of sympathy, frustration, kindness, politeness, supportiveness, or sarcasm.

It can be no more than social laughter, i.e. laughing on cue when a laugh is expected by someone saying something that s/he believes is funny.

Oh! Ho! Ho! Ha! Ha! Smirk. Smile. Slap. "Good one." Wink-wink; nudge-nudge; know what I mean? It's a gesture toward something not perceived as a jest.

At one point in my twenties, I tend to respond to this type of faulty punchline speaking by saying, "That's so funny that I'm going to write it down... and throw it away."

Much more recently, in Winnipeg, I see a few good actors wasting their talents with some less talented ones in an improv group that's performing a very poorly done "comedic" play that has no funny scenes or moments.

Later, after a late meal, I ask my cousin Kaeren what she thinks of the play. All she can say is "weird". She has a good sense of humour. She's being kind.

During the play, while waiting fruitlessly until the last line for something to laugh about, it's easy to tell that there is a group of uncritical, insincere, or desperate supporters of the cast in the audience. These are shills?

That group laughs long and loudly after almost every not-funny and punchless line in the play.

I don't know whether that softens the blow for the cast, of sensing that the audience isn't amused, or if the faked and unmerited laughter makes the embarrassment of the cast feel worse.

It reminds me of a public meeting that I attend a couple of decades earlier, in Vancouver, wherein the audience, which is unwilling to listen to a critical questioner, applauds over her voice to silence her.

In Winnipeg, the intent of the loud laugh feigning is clearly the opposite, but the lack of sincere interest is parallel.

The loud laughter isn't a response to any funny lines on stage because there aren't any. It's laughing over instead of applauding over, with the opposite intents.

When I'm trying to find an official definition of laughter, I find one dictionary entry defining laughter as an involuntary, spontaneous muscular reaction to a humourous stimulus. This is what I call real or authentic laughter.

If you can't help but laugh, something funny is going on.

The stimuli can be aural, including subtle or blunt jokes; visual, such as comic behaviour in real life or on film; or physical, such as tickling.

From personal experience, I would include situational. There are some situations which make me laugh inside or out loud, from recent and more distant events.

This would include organizing some audio-visual materials in alphabetical order backward and 1) not realizing the mistake until finishing; and 2) realizing that no one else ever notices the mistake. It's a true story.

This is also unintended humour which still makes me laugh.

Another personal instance of authentic laughter is the after laugh.

It happens when I don't understanding a joke when I first hear it, but some years later, when I finally do get it, I suddenly start laughing in front of completely different people.

Whenever this happens, I either have to say, "I just thought of something funny, nothing really. I'll tell you later, when you forget that I was laughing."

Otherwise, I have to tell the joke myself and explain to the people around me why I suddenly start laughing for no apparent, immediate reason.

Authentic laughter that's provoked in ways such as these has noticeable physical effects on the person laughing, the laugher.

Authentic laughter contorts facial features far beyond the effects of just smiling broadly or feigning laughter; makes internal organs jiggle ("like a bowl full of jelly"); distorts posture to a point that may appear to be deformation; and, can even cause eye-watering that's close to tears if not actual rolling tears.

My mom and other women of her generation tell me that very hearty laughter causes them to almost experience involuntary urination, even in their younger years.

A famous movie line goes further in defining real laughter. It says that sometimes we laugh because something is funny and sometimes we laugh because it's true.

During my evening of almost endless laughter in Toronto, I'm learning that the stimulus causing the laughing doesn't even have to be consciously perceived or apparent to the the laugher.

This may be the case in all of my volumes of humour.

But seriously reader, we also laugh when something is disconcerting. I make use of this laughter stimulus too.

### Criminally inane

During my first visits to Donnacona, I ask Denis Cantin to tell me the French translations of some gangster words.

He tells me about "la pégre" and "faire disparaître du monde".

This is long before my first months in Fukuoka, when I hear the ugly gringos espousing their conspiracy theories, paranoia, and their suspicions that a student saying he's a flourist is actually yakusa.

(Much later, the ugly gringos vote for and get the government they truly deserve, one reflecting their humourless mentality. Their president is a bad joke on the entire world.)

Humour can intrude upon even the most serious contexts, including language classes designed to enable and enhance clear and simple communication.

Notwithstanding the not-really-yakusa flourist, I have a recurring humourous urge to teach students how to comprehend and communicate clearly with stereotypical criminals, as depicted in popular fiction, print and video.

Inspired by Raymond Chandler and a host of actors portraying the archtypical toughies, I daydream about teaching English language students how to talk with them.

This is irresistibly mischievous and just thinking about it causes me to experience authentic laughter.

The potential misunderstandings are the stuff of the most successful situation comedies.

Students will first have to unlearn the familiar and more commonplace uses of words and combinations of words such as contract, hit, rub out, concrete, overcoat, and let them have it.

The humour of this teaching comes when the student tries to use "gangster" language skills in non-criminal conversations.

If the student adopts the stereotypical accents often associated with the word usage, especially when talking to someone unfamiliar with or not expecting such usage, the results could be worthy of double-takes and gasps.

Imagine a second language learner speaking with an accent having nothing to do with his/her first language.

Maybe we could teach students how to speak with Italian, Russian, Spanish, or other accents to benefit from the mythical and defamatory stereotypes of popular anglophone entertainment that far too often depicts people with those accents as criminals.

Adding an out-of-place accent is much funnier than a person who is inept in English priding her/himself on being able to say "gonna" or "gotta" in the middle of poorly spoken English.

And imagine the reactions of a second language learner to anglophones innocently using some of the same words used in "gangster" language.

A non-violent "gangster" language learner applying for employment requiring skill in the English language might be reluctant to work for a potential employer offering "a contract".

If the student isn't dissuaded and mentions the term "rub out", the employer might perceive the student as asking for an amendment to the contract.

After getting the job, if the student encounters a courier picking up a parcel, what might happen if the student's supervisor says "Let him have it."?

Some confusion may arise in the mind of a "gangster" language learner while reading about a snuff box in some account of times past.

The "gangster" language learner might wonder if it's a weapon or a coffin for the snuffed.

Likewise the expression about making someone disappear from the face of the Earth.

Is this about a crime, climate change, a space shot, or a magic show?  Yes, climate change is a crime against all life.

And abracadabra does have a sound which could be misheard as macabre cadaver.

Will the "gangster" language learner assume that a gangster is being honoured at a grad school convocation when s/he is summoned to get the "third degree"?

The gangster is a PhD candidate?

When a "gangster" language learner is asked simple questions in ordinary social settings, "gangster" vocabulary could make simple communication hilariously confusing or even frightening for some anglophones encountering the student.

The question, "What's your name?" could be answered with "Who's asking?", "Who wants to know?", and/or, "Are you a nark or a snitch?"

Despite "text books" favoured by phoney language teachers and language business establishments (l.b.e.), there are some questions that are rarely asked and answered.

But what might happen if a "gangster" language learner is asked these questions?

"Do you have any brother and sisters?" is a favourite question of the "text books".

It's a weird question to ask, out of the blue, to someone you are meeting for the first time, unless you are both small children repeating what adults ask you all the time, to show or patronizingly feign interest in talking to you.

In my personal experience, I know some people for many years before I find out whether or not they have siblings. In many cases, I still don't know and never ask.

What does it matter?

We have mutual interests and talk about them. We're getting to know each other as people, not as representatives of some biological kinship group.

The "gangster" language learning can discourage the sibling question by saying:

"Are you heat?  You don't want to know my family.  The first time might be your last."

An even more bizarre "text book" question, implying an intimacy that's very rare among complete strangers is: "How old are you?"

This one merits a "gangster" language reply, such as:

"I don't know how old you are, but one more question like that and I'll be asking you if you want to live until your next birthday!"

The far more common and much easier to deal with social question: "What do you do?", has an obvious "gangster" language retort: "I'm a legitimate business person."

To add a bit of confusion to the at least potentially scary answer, a female "gangster" language learner could say, "businessman".

An alternative answer and conversation ender is: "I do contract work.  Do you want to take out a contract on someone?"

This could help a female "gangster" language learner to distance herself from an annoying macho sexist male.

If he doesn't take her seriously, a likely reaction from this type of person, he might quip back: "I'd like to take you out."

Her counter-punch is to reply: "If you don't scram, I'll take you out, permanently."

For the more obnoxious macho suitor, who suggests going for a drive together, the reply could be: "So, you want to go for a little ride, do you? You'd never come back."

To fend off other unwanted attention in a beverage lounge, the question "What are you drinking?" can be countered with: "What's it to ya!"

To stereotypical questions, such as "Haven't I seen you before?" and "Do you come here often?", the obvious reply is: "Ask my shyster lawyer."

To the more persistent posers of unwelcome questions, someone far too nosy, the "gangster" language learner could respond: "You ask a lot of questions. Are you wired? Are you an undercover agent?"

If the questioner turns out to be a dimwit sexist macho male who picks up on only the word "undercover" and runs with it, the "gangster" language learner could say, "How would you like to go to sleep permanently?"

Shopping in a department store could get nasty if a "gangster" language learner offers to buy an overly-pushy clerk "a pair of cement overshoes" or "a cement overcoat".

At a waterside vacation resort, where the sellers of boat tours get too aggressive, a "gangster" language learner could say, "How would you like to go on a trip to the bottom of the water?"

In a fishing village, the inhabitants could mistake the "gangster" language learner as a reluctant fisher who dabbles in lobster trapping when s/he talks of being sent up the river to the slammer.

We could teach students to say all of the above, but maybe we would "never get away with it"; be "surrounded" by students who couldn't quite learn it; and come out of classes with our "hands up" in frustration, shouting, "So you won't talk, eh!"

## Disorganized crime

Police officers shown in popular entertainment sometimes say that only they are the professionals. The criminals are not.

So all criminals are amateurs, i.e. they commit crimes for enjoyment, not for income?

Most crime is disorganized, particularly after a raid and arrests. If crime were organized, there would be no prison inmates.

Disorganized crime could also describe the outcome of work attempted by inept, incompetent, corrupt, manipulative, and overly intrusive bureaucracy, especially pedantocracy.

It spends generations maliciously swindling taxpayers through lifelong employment income and generous pension plans.

## Too good to be false

When Mariko and I have our living as a newcomer in Tokyo experience, I find out that I can get free Japanese language classes at one of the ward halls.

The only apparent qualification is to live or work in that ward. Since I'm all over the city every day, I qualify.

The stickler is the individual interview that every applicant for the course has to attend. A panel decides whether an applicant can enrol in the course.

I imagine that this is just a formality for most applicants. They appear before the panel and it determines that they have no language skills at all. So they're accepted.

My appearance before the panel is more challenging. I have to convince them that I need the course. Since I can say what I say well in Japanese, the panel is sceptical.

It's a challenge for me because I have a history of knowing how to make myself understood regardless of my abilities or lack thereof in the language surrounding me.

Mariko is always amazed and amused by what I can convey to others, especially the long way 'round that I use for getting across a message.

## Discovery of Colombian misproportions

After my first months in Rio de Janeiro, I visit some neighbouring countries, including Paraguay.

I know little of that country before arriving, being only vaguely familiar with the fact that Guaraní is the most widely spoken language, followed by Español.

Guarani is a First Nations language.

When I arrive in Assución, I notice that the population seems to include many people of Asian origin. Some tell me they're Chinese from Taiwan.

They own many of the rundown local hotels. But I see only Español and Guaraní languages posted in most places, not Chinese.

In fact, I only know that the signs are in unfamiliar script which I presume is Guaraní. I'm illiterate in Guaraní. I can't read any of the signs in Guaraní writing.

What I perceive as Guaraní appears to be an Asian-like script, which misleads me to believe that I'm making a major discovery.

Here's the most remarkable evidence I ever see, showing the long-term historical ties between the peoples of Asia and the Americas.

The migrations from the eastern part of Asia are evidenced by the Guaraní script that I'm seeing in Assución. Wow!

But I'm wrong. The completely unfamiliar script is Korean. Naikũmbýi!... ndaha'éi guarani.

### Unimpaired vision

If a gay person becomes very angry does that mean he <u>can</u> see straight?

Does a gay person have to go to an orthodontist to fix straight teeth?

Only straight people can become dangerously crazy. That's why there are no gayjackets.

## Tranquility base

If you must talk to yourself, please use telepathy.

## Scratch achooo!

Allergy sufferers need a pollenectomy. Avoid pollenesia. Don't eat pollenta. Refrain from attending a pollenytechnical institute.

## Cartoon songs

I have yet to see a woman confined to lifelong domestic chores singing "Whistle while you work", as depicted in a U.S. animated feature film made long before my birth.

I can hardly imagine standing up in a mining crew bus before dawn and leading a singalong of "Hi Ho Hi Ho. It's off to work we go." and getting a "Happy" reception.

Yet that too is the message in the same cartoon movie.

I'm wondering if another song from that cartoon should translate into French as: "Samedi mon prince viendra."

It implies a much more precise knowledge of a desired future event than the uncertain English lyrics.

But as someone famous who does actually marry a prince soon discovers, it's better not to become a member of a royally racist family.

## Restless

I write to Rev. Jennifer in concern one day when I realize it's "Sunday", the seventh day in her religionism's "week", also called, "a day of rest".

Aside: Yet the calendars based on her religionism show "Sunday" as the first day of the week!  We now return to our story:

Although "Sunday" is now a work day for most retail businesses in many of the nation-states that I know, one's sharing Jennifer's religionism, and probably some other nation-states that I don't know too, this open door policy is still resisted in some localities.

Some include Lustagoocheehk.  There, the churchist religionists still manage to keep at least one large supermarket closed on Sunday mornings.

This half day of rest gives the religionist employed time to attend religionist meetings.

Non-religionists simply get a free morning to waste by sleeping so that they can be refreshed for their employer.

Opposition to allowing retailers to open on Sundays is billed as "family time", but people who get a day off or sleep off a day don't necessarily spend it with family.

Thinking of Rev. Jennifer and her counterparts in the same type of religionism on this particular Sunday, I finally realize that they have to work today.

So I write another tongue-in-cheek note to Jennifer about this situation.

As a supporter of labour unions and a political party long financed by them, this should concern her.

I write:

You are in one of the rare salaried occupations that's never getting a day off on Sunday. Even supermarket shift workers get that day off sometimes.

Have you and your colleagues ever considered forming a union to negotiate with your boss for a day of rest?

Not a prayer?

Would such a union be called CBU, cloth bearers union: SDU, sermon deliverers union; SLU, spiritual leaders union, or what?

## ...in bad faith

The employeed asks for a salary increase but the employer offers only unwanted advances.

## Walking dogs & children

We pass the s.i.e.* Sisyphus people on the sidewalks of this city. My pronunciation of s.i.e. as sigh. Here, they're out on their routine time walks.

(*standard issue existence)

Some are following dogs' bowel and bladder schedules. Others are following children who crave variety in life.

Too many others are following schedules learned from employers who treat them like dogs and children for too many years.

## Edgy

It's been a while since I see a sign beside a sidewalk ordering people to "curb your dog". The edge of a sidewalk is now more commonly used by governments and economists. In all cases, perhaps, the objective is to prevent an unrestrained outpouring and depositing outcome which risks to spread everywhere and soil everything.

## Come on

The desired outcome isn't always attainable through the desired income. I concentrate on outcome.

## Comic relief

Jokes and humour just pop into my head spontaneously at unpredictable moments. They don't appear in my writing for a purpose, such as breaking up a very serious section.

Besides, comic relief is simply a social welfare programme for humorous people.

Or is it sitting in a toilet reading the funny papers?

## Intox humour

Riding a highway bus between Niagara Falls and Toronto, I notice much roadside advertising for a variety of purveyors of alcoholic grape juice makers.

One catching my eye more than others calls itself "Organized Crime Winery". Is this like posting video of your illegal activities on the internet?

## Disturbing stories

In his book <u>Les Années d'Impatience</u>, Gérard Pelletier says that Pierre Trudeau "dérangait tout le monde" throughout his life. It's a positive comment. He makes people think.
It's interesting that the French word "déranger" is used in negative senses to indicate mental illness in English. Anglophones call people "deranged" and "disturbed".

In an age when climate change is largely ignored and no decisive immediate action is taken to stop it, deranging and disturbing governments and people is an essential public service.

Since my late teens, when other students and co-workers apologize for "disturbing" me, I always tell them not to be concerned because "I'm already disturbed."

## Assaulting

The only respectful and desirable cavity search is performed by a dentist.

Compulsory military service leads to unwanted attention and non-consensual behaviour.

## Crimes against inanity

While living in Ottawa, I subject my acquaintances to so much word play that they could rightly accuse me of capital punishment.

## One liners (without any type of Ester)

A put on is not a wearable garment.

Goats don't joke, but they're kidding.

Holding a Laugh-In, until it bursts out.

When is the hour of humour?

What is the atomic structure of matter that laughs?

Headline: UFO brings being funny.

### Ban all

In an age when "redacting", i.e. censoring public documents and removing books and knowledge from libraries and classrooms is becoming prevalent, banning is nothing new.

There is a much longer history of banning involving a broad spectrum of things in life, such as al, jo, dana, yan, shee, nock, nerol, king, deau, dit, to, nister, quette, er, ner, derlog, ish, tam, ter, and zai.

### Transport getting nowhere

A carport must be a building for boarding an automobile.

Carpool: polluted

Boathouse for sale: no sink.

### Unmelodious silence

Tune up: hum and purrfect; flying grooved discus

Tune out: old songs

Out of tune: radio silence caused by fragile slipped discs or missing discs

Off tune: not a hit

Tone deaf: silent alarm

Tone down: tenor or base

Jam session: delayed, unsweetened sticky annoyed commuter

Strike up the band: abruptly tighten loose cloth sweat absorber

Discussion: sound impact; ear damage caused by wave blow

Clarinet: casting around instead of visionary

Trumpet: inedible crumpet

Trombone: anatomically incompatible

Percussion: struck by sonic cat

Drum out: damaged during outdoor concert

Cymbals: meaningless clatter

String section: third floor

Wind section: broken glass or open air

Pipes: full of holes and leaking squeaking sounds

Bagpipes: defective and discarded plumbing

Sound argument: inedible taste; disagreement

Hit parade: gauntlet run

## Colourless

Yellow peril: dangerous jaundice or hepatitis 3

Red purge: diarrhea

White power: pale, washed out, bleached

Garbage pale: white power; shocked by wasteful
Obesity: waist of food

Blues: aqua, navy, dark, pale, sky

Green piece: kiwi slice; camouflaged firearm

Orange aid: carrot or mandarin farm worker

Violet: small fiddle

## Half baked

Studebaker: studious one or prolific with progeny

Rutabaga: impolite

## Bald lie

Barbarian: racist coiffeur master

## Old Bailey whack

Cited for contempt of court?

## Unprofitable humour

The last laughs on me, but only if you can take paypal, cheques, or credit cards.

Getting no credit for hard work means your credit card application is rejected or your card is declined.

Can you cash in on something in a cashless world?

NSF check means no security force.

A credit cheque and rating is the work of a sceptical cashier.

Canada must be a paradise for the sex industry due to Johnny Cake and the Johnny Cash Machines at one trust company.

Canada has no nuclear weapons and yet it once has ABMs. In such a frigid climate, cash would be warmer if the machines were set higher.

Perhaps it could be put into the dryer longer too, after coming out of crypto states and gangs.

The crypto adhere to a religionism of invisibility.

Cryptography is the money shot, if cryptogenic.

Cryptocurrency involves old news posing as new.

It's no secret that shocking outcomes can lead the crypto to the crypt. They suffer from cryptococcocis and need to divest through cryptotherapy and cryptosurgery.

## Couplings

Shipmate: sea spouse

Roommate: recluse

Running mate: fleeing spouse

Amalgamate: spouse with overextended family

Housemate: garage

Stalemate: one who becomes boring due to over-familiarity or two people who lose interest in each other

Ahoy Métis! a drift or out to see what's running

Happily married: moneyed couple without children, mortgage, payments, and debts (That's why they're moneyed!)

## Money grove

"Money is the root of all evil". It perches on the branches of banks, stems consumer spending, blossoms in possessions, and leaves you unfulfilled.

So it must grow on trees after all.

## Regimen

When the dentist begins explaining the procedure about to begin, I interrupt by saying "I know the drill."

## Whirled news

Restrictions on South African traveller's wishing to go abroad, after the S.A. nation-state announced the discovery of a new COVID-19 variant, are pandemic Apartheid.

So is restricting the circulation of vaccines against this virus to the "first" world European-centered nation-states.

The U.S. states' anti-abortion laws and the U.S. supreme court's decision to abolish women's right to choose whether or not to abort a pregnancy amount to Taliban rule.

## More and less

The opposite of homeless is homemore in the sense of more than anyone actually needs.

While many people struggle to survive in city streets, others live in housing that far exceeds their numbers and practical shelter needs.

The homemore spend more on decorations, renovations, and remodelling than the homeless can hope to receive in food aid for many years.

## Girdling

The interestingly shaped buildings of the northern outskirts of old Metro Toronto, where the GO buses move quickly and unobstructed by car traffic, remind me of something.

Oh yes.  The era when European-era women are forced to girdle themselves so that they can't breathe easily and think straight.  It's a female-only straightjacket of sorts.

The buildings of the outskirts are corsettes.

Perhaps the underlying intent of the girdle-like structures that I see from the GO bus is to stifle humanity until it is gasping for life and doesn't know why.

### Wordliness

I grow up in an almost expletive free household and immediate family, so I'm not inclined to use expletives at all.

The main reason that they sometimes creep into my voice is the extreme overuse of them in U.S. movies, for no apparent reason.

Shock value and comic relief are long gone.  It seems to be imposed by the movie companies or a sign of lazy writing.

In my household and family I never hear almost anyone saying anything resembling a curse word, swearing, and the like, particularly toward or describing other people.

The two exceptions in expletive usage are my grandad Jack and his younger daughter, my mom.

Grandad Jack's expletives are two words which churchist religionists probably call blasphemy.  When my maternal grandad gets annoyed he says "God Damnit".

The only time I hear this word is when he's defending me from anyone trying to manipulate me, particularly my maternal grandma.

"Leave the Godamn kid alone!" Grandad Jack shouts to his spouse.

My mom says "the s word" so rarely that I don't recall any particular incident of her using it. When I catch her she stops.

That's it.

Even my older paternal cousins, who my mom dismisses as inferior to her, use no expletives in my presence. Perhaps they use them in their work or at home.

Two work in the military and in "rough" employment.

My dad never uses expletives, despite his six years away from home, mainly living in military bases during wartime and perhaps among routine expletive users. I don't know.

My dad always refers to expletives as an indication of a lack of vocabulary in the person using them.

My elementary school experience may confirm his assertion.

School children in that institution have limited vocabularies and the first time I hear expletives outside my household and immediate family are in elementary school.

I only recall one kid using an expletive and only when agitated by one particular word, "farmer". I presume that his family farmed and other kids looked down on farmers.

Why have such a negative opinion of people who provide everything that we eat?

Whenever addressed as "farmer" he would instantly reply with "the f word", indicating that it applied to his tormentor.

Such expletives are also called "four letter words" in English.

Only two four letter words are the most common that I hear in U.S. movies and more common usage during my years among the anglophones.

It's ironic that people who get paid to write scripts assume that it's okay to bore audiences by only writing two words and variations thereof.

It's cheap shot, fast laugh "humour".

At a movie theatre matinee in Toronto filled with children, all the kids burst into laughter at the single use of only one of the two words. Audiences are treated like children?

Are the writers or their bosses showing a low opinion of the audience; dumbing down the audience; or just too lazy to write a variety of words for the audience?

There's a difference between reflecting or catering to an audience; edifying an audience by exposing it to unfamiliar vocabulary; and, repeatedly conditioning an audience, like brainwashing, by writing only two words.

The two words are "the f word" and the "the s word".

The first is a vulgar euphemism for excrement. The second is a vulgar but in some contexts widely used synonym for coitus.

I understand why excrement gets abused, but why love-making?

As used, or abused, the "s" and "f" words substitute for "very" or for portraying something or someone negatively.

One of my elderly cousins attacks my dad with one of these words at Granny Mary's funeral, saying my dad is excrement.

It is an unmerited and inaccurate description of my dad, his character, and his behaviour toward others.

He is a much loved and respected person who is considered someone who can do no wrong or harm, an authentic gentleman whose chief character flaw is sometimes being too selfless toward people he loves.

The elderly cousin maligning my dad is angry because he says that he didn't know Granny Mary was about to die and my dad didn't tell him. My dad is a god to my cousin?

Many of us almost believe that Granny Mary is immortal because of her longevity, but we should all realize that she is actually mortal. She's nearly 103 when she dies.

I'm sorry to see her go and I miss her, but I'm not surprised or angry with anyone. She tells me a year earlier, and many times before then, that she wants to go.

She dies by millimetres, as my dad puts it. She does not fall ill or suffer from a prolonged illness.

Her gradual and eventual demise is in no way sudden and should surprise no one.

I know it will happen eventually and sooner than later. I don't hang around waiting for anyone to die. I'm not morbid. I'm alive, so I try to live a fulfilling life.

I'm Granny Mary's living legacy, not a demobilized or paralyzed mourner-in-waiting.

I'm thousands of kilometres away at her time of death.

I don't make a frantic dash to "say goodbye", spending a fortune on last-minute transportation to show off the fact that I care and will spare no expense to prove it by showing up for the final breath.

Dying people who truly love you don't want you to make your life more difficult by going into debt or hardship just to say "goodbye".

The same applies to showing intense emotions and feelings towards a dead corpse. I don't go to funerals after reaching adulthood.

Crying at a funeral seems like self pity grief, at best. Dead people don't see or hear you weeping. They gain nothing from your postmortem, all-too-late tears.

You're crying for yourself or to prove your love of the corpse to other survivors? That does nothing for the dead. They see, hear, touch, and feel nothing coming from you.

What's the point of showing love and respect for anyone when s/he's dead or when you're dead? My dad asks me this question while he's still alive.

It's more fitting to remember what the deceased does right while living, and to consider it model behaviour to try to emulate.

Imagining, instead, that the dead benefit from loving and extravagant attention, followed by years of visits to their rotting corpses or bottled dust, is simply kidding yourself.

It's more than likely self-serving behaviour to stave off some strange feelings of guilt about a death not caused because you committed murder.

Ceremonializing and monumentalizing death is the same joke that the pharaohs of Egypt play on the slave labourers who suffer and die building pyramids for the dead bodies of monarchical dictators.

The more grotesque joke is slaughtering "servants" and others to bury with the dictators.

It's the harshest form of the same joke at someone else's expense that is paid for by struggling taxpayers when they are obliged to finance lavish ceremonies, huge monuments, and elaborate graves for unelected and elected heads of nation-states.

It's a sarcastic way of making fun of the deceased's mourners and the deceased simultaneously.

How could any mourner say, with a straight face, "Oh, I forgot to show you that I love you while you were alive. Is it too late now?"

And yet some mourners do exactly that, in effect, after the body goes cold.

The elder cousin attacking my dad at Granny Mary's funeral isn't demonstrating his capacity for loving anyone, particularly not my grandma, who is my dad's mother.

What a sick joke.

The elderly cousin's bitter and emotional outburst and diatribe against my dad at Granny Mary's funeral demonstrate only that the elderly cousin has no respect for my dad and his mother.

My dad is not responsible for Granny Mary's age, death, or for the fact that the elderly cousin does not visit her often and does not frequently and routinely contact the institution where she's staying to check on her well-being.

The elderly cousin is merely, unwittingly, expressing his lifelong need for help.

Instead of getting help, he mocks himself by wasting years of energy letting his bitterness churn inside him for a lifetime because his father, one of my dad's oldest brothers, leaves his spouse during the elderly cousin's childhood.

After the elderly cousin's father dies, in his 80s, the elderly cousin needs someone else to lash out against and my dad is the only target in proximity.

The elderly cousin illustrates that psychological issues, as well as blind, ignorant, self-destructive, and humourless anger is the source of much of the use of "four letter words".

These are words of frustration and blaming other people or things for unpleasant experiences and personal failures.

There are so many ordinary words that are more severe and appropriate that it's difficult to understand why excrement and love-making are more commonly used.

Imagine calling someone excrement or love-making. It sounds silly and doesn't make any sense. It renders the speaker incomprehensible and laughable.

"My love-making pen has gone dry." Pens have sex?

"What an excrement day!" Feces are falling from the sky?

"My father is making love with my mother." So?

It's pathetic that the users of the "s" and "f" expletives don't know any of the huge assortment of more effective and emphatic words for criticizing others for actual misdeeds.

It's also boring to hear the same two words over and over again, particularly in a movie that you are paying people to write, produce, direct, and act in.

People who routinely, constantly, and repeatedly use expletives are boring, annoying, and denigrating. "Cela casse aux oreilles!"

It's like being asphyxiated by toxic fumes from a fossil fuel internal combustion engine or the toxic stinky breath of a nicotine junkie. It makes me desperate for fresh air.

Routinely, constantly, and incessantly using expletives completely neutralizes their mindless repetition and potential shock value.

It's like eating the same meal every day, three times a day, i.e. worse than prison rations?

Excessive expletive usage is worse than illiteracy and much like it. Excessive expletive usage is communicative incompetence in the saddest and most pathetic sense.

The users are to be pitied, not looked down upon, criticized, or condemned for vulgarity. The users are simply ignorant in an easily rectifiable sense.

If the users were capable of insulting others in a very clever way, that would stymie the people they were trying to insult and leave them puzzled by the insulting person's laughter.

The insulting person could use some of these phrases:

"I suggest that you emulate the reproductive behaviour of a single-celled life form called amoeba."

(I actually do advise someone to use this line at one time.)

"May I suggest that you order a dish that features e-coli?

"Hmm, on second thought, perhaps you have already consumed a sufficient quantity of this type of unsavoury victual to satiate every pore in your body.

"You epitomize that which you consume in excess."

"I remain as unsympathetic to your plight as a fecal sample left out to dry and harden in the summer sun."

"You bear a strong resemblance to the lowest orifice of the human intestines."

"I have the impression that you are much like a human reproductive organ."

Imagine a man and woman insulting each other by calling each other the name of one of their sexual characteristics.

Why would that be an insult to anyone? How can it be considered obscene?

...

The sad state of people limited to only expletives inspires me to start creating a lexicon to help them to go beyond and expand their extremely restricted vocabulary of adjectives.

There are so many four letter words and so many of them are easy, common, and often nice words.

There are so many and varied combinations of these words that can be used to highly praise or severely criticize places, people, acts, and events.

Here's the resulting four letter word dictionary:

### Four

A: ally, axle, able, ache, arch, atom, auto, alum, amen, anon, anal...

B: born, baby, bark, bill, bold, ball, bait, boat, bear, bare, beer, bell, bind, belt, bred, brat, bite, burp, bald, bile, bong, butt, bate, blue, beep, bide, bomb, bolt, boar, bore, bend, bent, bump, bode...

C: cute, cure, coat, cane, calf, cool, crop, crop, core, crib, coin, care, card, cone, call, cape, cent, cope, coal, curt, chum, clot, clip, calm, clam, cake, cape, carp, cell, chin, chit, chug, clod, clog...

D: deal, deed, deet, door, dale, date, dean, dote, dose, duck, dive, duke, dine, done, down, drop, drip, doze, drug, drat, dung, dike, dirt, dent, dolt, dork, dart, dark, dupe, dune, darn, drat...

E: easy, ease, edge, even, ever, eyes, ears...

F: food, feed, fact, fame, fort, foot, feel, faze, fuel, free, fake, folk, foam, fret, flux, fate, font, food, felt, frog, fair, fare, fear, fell, fork, flog, flag, flip, fist, five, fire, fuse, fish, flop, fowl, fare, fain, fool, fate, foul, frat, flit, fume, four, film, fill, fuge, fold...

G: good, glow, goat, goad, gale, gear, gilt, gang, gate, gold, grid, goal, gill, guff, goof, grey, geld, geld, gild gain, glib, goer, gore, grip, glen, glum...

H: hope, hint, hive, heat, head, heed, hype, hoax, hate, hill, honk, hear, here, harp, help, harm, hilt, helm, hall, heal, heel, hell, holy, hole, hair, hurt, hour, harp, huge, hold, herd, hind, horn, hemp, halt...

I: iota, iron, item, itch...

J: joke, join, juke, jute...

K: keep, kept, keen, kill, kite, kilt, king, kiln, knee, keel...

L: live, love, loaf, lore, loan, like, lake, late, lean, lint, load, lead, leaf, lone, liar, luge, loss, lair...

M: milk, meek, meow, main, moat, more, mean, male, mail, mane, mute, moan, mitt, mite, mole, mill, many...

N: name, note, nape, nose, nine, noon, neon, neck, neat, nuke, nark, node, near...

O: oink, omen, ooze, only, oral, open, oxen...

P: pure, pine, pour, poor, pore, perk, pork, park, pier, pair, poet, pore, peal, post, pile, pale, pole, pull, pill, port, posh, pear, peer, pipe, prey, pray, perm, pimp, plum, push...

Q: quip, quit, quiz, quad...

R: roar, real, read, rust, rote, rate, ruin, rite, rise, root, rack, rock, rare, rink, rear, reed, ripe, rake, rose, roar, rope, ring, role, roll, rail, rule, riot, rill, romp, reap, rich, rust, race, rent, road, rode...

S: silk, silt, soak, sick, salt, such, shot, stop, stir, show, shop, soap, seed, sand, sock, sell, sold, soft, slid, slot, star, seal, size, sing, sign, song, soul, sole, sear, sill, seem, send, sent, slim, stud, stem, slip, sled, slow, slaw, soda, sump, sore, soak, send, soil...

T: trip, tape, trip, take, talk, tear, toll, tint, type, trap, toot, text, twit, twin, team, time, trek, tame, toot, torn, tune, tame, tilt, tell, trot, tube, thud, thug, tram, trim, term, till...

U: unit, unto, undo, ugly, umbo, upas, upon, urea, uric, urus, user...

V: vast, vase, vine, vote, vain, vile, veal, volt, veil, vale, vain, vein, veld, vent, very, vary, vert, vest, veto, viol, visa, vice, viva, void, vair, vang...

W: wise, wish, walk, word, work, well, will, warm, week, weak, wood, wool, weed, wolf, wave, wain, wane, wage, wink, worn, wear, with, want, what, when, wake, wick, wipe, watt, wail, wale, weld, wilt, welt, wife, weft, wane, wisp, wire, wiry, wist, wand, wonk, warp, wrap, wren, wimp...

X: Xmas, xray...

Y: yore, yell, yard, yarn, year, yeah, yegg, yoga, yogi, yoke, yowl, your, yule, yurt, yank, yawl, yawn, yolk, ylem, yelp...

Z: zest, zoom, zeal, zing, zone, zany, zero, zinc, zein, zizz, zonk, zouk, zori...

## Flagrant fragrance

My observations indicate that in the U.K. and at least some other European countries in the same "longitude" area, the "unwashed masses" is an apt description of a cross-section of the inhabitants, including the elite.

Consequently, according to legend, the elite are the ones who finance, promote, and use perfumes to hide the stench of their unwashed bodies.

Thus perfumes become celebrated, renowned, and yearned for by so many, including the non-elite with larger disposable incomes or people in debt.

Elite smell. Elite do. Others do too.

## Stationary place

The U.K. caste system in which a tiny, classless, moneyed, crude minority elite play the role of self-obsessed exploiters who impoverish and render unfulfilling the equally crude non-elite, refers to the resulting relative well-being and lack thereof as "one's station in life."

The caste system is so tight that the chances of leaving the station are extremely low, if not nil. Tickets out are hard to come by.

Working very hard does not ensure departure from non-elite status, as I observe in the "third" world.

Now this writing, originally from notes desperately written down, is likely to come across as something like a shaggy dog story.

All this introduction is simply to introduce some humour.

Moles Station is on the Arres Station line. Ge Station may not turn out to be humourous.

### Amateur nouns

Or should this section be titled I pronounce you "he and she", "she and she", or "he-he"?

So a divorce is a result of mispronunciation?

During the brief, Iraq-U.S. led, N.A.T.O.-C.C.C.P. war against Iraq's invasion of Kuwait, the U.K. news readers and reporters turn the invaded nation-state into a waiting line.

In the same reportorial parlance, Uruguay becomes you. What's a guay?

### I'm more Japanese?

As we leave Hakata station on a day trip, I'm looking at the kiosk and recalling that tiny bottles of milk and hard-boiled eggs are standard fare at such places during my first and second times in Nippon.

I tell Mariko that I want to go to the kiosk today and ask the seller if s/he has those two items. I say that it will be amusing if the seller is too young to know what I mean.

But the train leaves before I can go and ask.

I recall having to explain to a much younger clerk in a Canadian camera shop the meaning of the word "slide". I wonder what younger generations think "slide show" means.

On the return trip to Sawaraku, just before boarding the chikatetsu, it occurs to me that when I first arrive in Nippon our friend Megumi has yet to be born.

Aboard the subway car, I look around and say to Mariko that most of the people aboard aren't born when I first visit Nippon.

So I know more about Nippon than most of the passengers in the car.

Mariko laughs, but things change so much since my first arrival that the other passengers would not know the country that I see at age 19.

### I'm the excuse

Mariko tells me many times over the years that I am the excuse for whatever she wants to do and doesn't want to do in Nippon.

She no longer has to explain herself to others here when she wants to opt out.

They assume it's because she's with me, a non-local with no strings attached to local social or cultural traditions or obligations.

It's perfect and removes all stress from Mariko and all frustrations with her from others.

I don't need any excuse anywhere to opt in and out of whatever I please. I dismiss conventions, which is a key point in all Terrian Journals writings.

### Nippon Post's tiny secret

It's the perfect gift for someone who bugs you. I see an advertisement for an insectarium in a post office and assume it's only a mascot or pet at the branch.

But when I'm looking for post office ads with typical local motifs that I can send abroad I find myself dealing with a can of worms, literally.

First I see an ad with a picture of worms on it. Mail a worm! We can ship the Canadian prime minister of the moment back to his ancestral home.

Then I think this is just some yuppie version of "the gift that keeps on giving".

I think the worms are silk worms. So a person can have a truly home spun life supply of fine material garments.

I look again and see moths. So the objective is to wear out clothes by having them moth-eaten?

Perhaps the bowl-of-bugs breakfast that I sample in Thailand, on the way from Singapura to Nippon, is becoming popular here too?

Finally I see other ads with more winged insects. Suddenly, I realize that I'm stumbling upon the secret explaining the efficiency of Nippon Post.

The one-day domestic postal service which the post office says will be improved by a new computer post office is neither an example of human nor technological competence.

Air mail doesn't wait at crowded airports with jammed runways.

The real secret is out. Japan Post uses flying insects to transport mail.

What genius! The bugs have tiny wire clips, shown in the ads, which are surgically inserted into the mid-wing area.

Now I also know why I only see one cockroach in a Fukuoka back lane during my now total two years and six months in Nippon.

Roaches and other beetles are surface mail carriers. What else could move the mail so fast at such low cost?

Another theory is that since caretaker society children must never be contaminated by earth, trees, bushes, water, etc. and must never know that wild lifeforms exist and can flourish without need of caretaker society, the post office has to appear to be the source and guarantor of all life.

But actually, Mariko tells me, after having a laughing fit from my theories, the bug ads are all about local schooled children.

They'll put pins through the winged ones for science projects. The school mid-year break and the calendar year end break are the seasons for giving bugs.

Insects for children are only one gift among cookies, mochi, drinks, etc., all in the usual, fancy, beautiful packaging.

Of course the bugs are packed separately.

The non-insect gifts are for people who are kind to you or for people who you owe allegiance or obedience to, Mariko explains. Children?

### Liars & lairs

Mariko practices Aikido with a Brasileiro named Lair. That is pronounced La Ir, like Ia cir. Only Mariko says his name correctly. Anglophones call him liar.

In the sport of golf, players sometimes have a reputation for cheating as well as lying about their scores.

In golf there are good and bad lies. Neither are true or false. Good lies are the source of compliments. Bad lies are a source of sympathy or competitive satisfaction.

What's more puzzling is the more general usage of lies.

A person lies down when s/he's laid up. But s/he does not lie up when laid down. It appears that some people cannot lie up. There are limits to lying?

More confusing in some vocabulary circles is the fact that a meal can be laid on a table and yet not laid.

Patient people can lie in waiting. Why aren't they truthful? How can some of them be so hazardous if they are only lying?

"Now I lay me down to sleep." seems like an impossibility, unless it is accomplished by a single-celled form of life.

I only know of certain creatures which can literally "lay in wait". The result is less weight for them.

Only the religionists could come up with a term like "layman". Is this someone who has sleeping sickness or who doesn't want to be active in life?

Or is a "layman" merely someone who is always lying?

The child-like expression "Liar, liar, pants on fire." is obviously inaccurate. How could anyone remain horizontal in the event of such a conflagration?

A brick layer lies in a brick lair devouring layers of cake.

A lay away plan is the same as a lay home plan. Both are laying about.

A layabout and a lie about can be essentially the same.

Chuang Hwa once has a government official who must be the victim of accusations every time that his name is spoken: Chou En Lai.

...

The U.S. won't sign the international treaty making it responsible for atrocities and all war crimes committed by it's military.

Even if it signs, its credibility will be in question from the outset because its previous governments try to deny the obvious: "Mi Lai".

...

When some people claim to be fond of something, or someone, remember the pronunciation of the first part of the word like.

...

Can big cats be trusted?  Maybe jaguars, tigers, etc. but the king of big cats is forever stigmatized by its name.

...

People involved in accidents and other mishaps try to explain claims to their insurance agents.

Sometimes the success of an insurance claimant to get a return from the premiums paid is decided by liability.

Can anyone ever say or know what actually happens if insurance is judged by such a potentially nonfactual deciding factor?

...

An often repeated, widely believed, and perhaps provable statement is reliable, whether true or not.  Credibility comes from reliability?

This puts the whole concept of "reliable source" into question.

...

This topic is better laid to rest?  Lime?

## Review

Music critics don't always write harmonious musical notes.

Critics need to take a sober second look after talking among themselves at cocktail parties.  It's time to re-read, re-listen, and re-view first impressions.

## Leading questioned

Leadership is a flotilla of one thing leading to another.

## État d'arrestation

Someone can be under arrest but not over.

Does an arrest warrant lead to a warranted arrest?

Some people need a rest?  But others need not arrest?

If you charge it will that result in hard times?

An example of arrested development could be a pipeline.  It becomes a pipe dream or nightmare

A pipeline is an assembly line for making wind musical instruments supported or opposed by hearing or blocked by a lack thereof.

When someone is detained someone else is retained.  Is the system tainted?

# Annuary

I'm working on a Japanese pun calendar, using alternate words to replace the numbers from one to twelve used in Nippon's modified version of the European calendar.

The first two months are difficult because I want to anglicize and rename them itchy and knee.

Then I realize that the number one has two alternative pronunciations in Japanese. It can be hitotsu. Does his enable me to rename the first month hiji or elbow month?

Ask me at that time.

Two can be futatsu, which can be called some type of hot month?

Three can be mitsu, which enables me to use the image of a famous singer.

Four can remain as shi, which is the name of a president of Chuang Hwa. How convenient. It's president's month.

Five is also the name of a game, go. So this is either game month or moving month.

Six is easy, ryoku, which can be mispronounced in English katakana and named for a ward of Rio de Janeiro that's called after the city.

Seven can be abbreviated from nana to the name of a Bharatanian bread.

Eight is bee month, hachi.

Nine is a martial arts level month.

Ten is pronounced ju, which can be renamed Star of David month.

Eleven and twelve months can accordingly become one and two stars of David respectively.

After my Japanese pun calendar is adopted, it will thus partly celebrate Judaism instead of some other religionisms.

Whatever the months are called, Fukuoka remains a hill of clothing, right?

### Bug toll

Typhoon 11, the first and last big storm of the climate changed typhoon season to actually hit our city this year, leaves us unscathed but it's harder on at least one insect.

In 11's aftermath, I find a dead cicada lying outside next to our laundry porch.

It's blown so far from home?

I'm only left wondering one thing: What's cada besides each?

### Weasel out

After one particularly strong rain storm, I hear a strange sound on an outside wall. It sounds like a snake so I tap on the wall to make sure it's not inside. No sound follows.

Then I look out a window and see a small brown creature dashing from one rice field to another too quickly for me to see a shape.

I assume it's a rat escaping drowning by irrigation.

Later the same day Mariko suddenly says, "What's that!" indicating something on our purple wall outside the laundry balcony window.

I don't know what it's called, but it might be a weasel. I get ample opportunity to look at it before it disappears over the edge and returns to the rice field.

We have a visitor, so I don't have a camera close beside me as I usually do. I have no picture of the creature.

There is a bushy tree beside the balcony. Could it be a mulberry bush? If so, do we need a monkey to chase the brown creature around the bush?

### Monkeying around

Mariko points out the obvious flaw in a widely used English language expression. It is "Monkey see. Monkey do."

The problem is singular versus plural form. At first I suggest that the expression is actually an s liaison. It's monkeys see...

But there is no "s" tailing the second monkey. Monkeys have "s"es, just like humans.

To be correct, the expression would have to be one of two possible choices: either monkeys see and monkeys do or monkey sees and monkey does.

Why does the originator of this expression not know English grammar? It's another often repeated mistake like the replaying of errors in pre-recorded news reports?

Monkeys must have evolved from humans?

This would derail the famous search for a "missing link" and result in an evolutionary train wreck.

Follow that link to your demise if you believe that humans are a divinely-created "superior" species destined to rule the world.

Please note that monkeys truly are more intelligent than humans.

Monkeys don't invent nuclear weapons, world war, or machines and weapons of mass pollution.

Nor do dinosaurs in all their 40 million year rule of Earth.

So where does that leave humans on the evolutionary scale? Rung zero or below?

Coal and petroleum are the dinosaur's and other long gone species' revenge for extinction.

Or are fossil fuels their means of restoring their planet to a hospitable state; making Earth inhabitable for them again; and creating environmental conditions that ready this planet for their triumphant return?

# Beyond drop off

A few years ago a social agency announces that people with unwanted infants can drop them off so that they can be placed with couples wanting children.

But some overly zealous adults who don't want to be parents are using this announcement as an excuse for dropping off children far beyond their infancy.

Only now does it dawn on me, aboard a flight from Sapporo to Fukuoka, that there's hope for unhappily married couples and disgruntled parents who realize, all too late, that they make a terrible mistake by having children and have given up all hope of correcting the incorrigible.

Without criminal acts or seriously endangering unwanted children's lives, repentant parents can free themselves of their children by making use of a public service long depicted in movies and TV as lifesaving, unjust, and/or undesirable.

In such entertainment, parents who actually do want to remain parents and care for their children are threatened by "social service" agents who try to take custody of the kids by force.

These agents can intervene and remove children from their parental homes under certain circumstances.

These agents do so for the children's "good", taking the kids from their parents' "care".

Using this type of social service, regretful and reluctant parents could set a situation in motion which would convince social service agents to remove the kids.

Parents could make anonymous reports to social service agencies indicating that their children need to be taken from their parents.

A regretful and reluctant parent support group could reinforce this type of report by working together as witnesses against each other.

In this way, both the parents and children would have potentially better futures.

The reluctant parents should remember to greet their childrens' removal with forlorn facial expressions and say, "I suppose it's for the best." And it certainly is that.

### Dear passengers

The Arabic and Japanese announcements are apparently comprehensible during our two flights, from Montréal to Doha and from Doha to Tokyo.

However there are no French announcements when we leave Montréal.

The English is also difficult to comprehend due to its apparently Arabic musical pronunciation.

This causes a reaction in my funny bone. My brain? I start to imagine announcements that could be made, based on the jargon used in routine flight announcements.

"Our in-flight menu includes a choice of bean dishes. Meal service may be suspended if we experience flatulence during the flight."

## Particulate matters

Are people in their nineties nanogenerians?  They shrink that much due to gravity?

## Alternative universalities

### Side bar

Turning in legal circles and seeing hopes go down the drain may be related to this term, making reference to a watering hole for barristers and solicitors.

This term might also reflect concern for people ascending and descending.

For others this term might represent helping others to fulfill a compulsive acquired need through the establishment of some affiliated business.

### Shikketori

I'm so critical of people who don't bother to learn languages when they enter the "outside" world, particularly anglophones.

Now I have to come clean about myself.  I'm a "remove humidity" repeat offender.  No shikketori isn't the name of some sort of bird or shrine gate.

Put simply, it's a small box of liquid with tiny round white orbs floating on top.  Humidity makes them disappear.

That's what I want to buy.  Since I don't seem to be able to find it I ask a clerk in the store.

I do this several times for a few years. I succeed in buying the box each time and in making Mariko laugh with me and at me.

I'm shopping in one of the stores where I buy other things over a period of years in Miyazaki and Fukuoka.

The encounter is something that somehow escapes me when I write my first two volumes of humour, <u>Terrian Journals' Jokes Nobody Gets</u> and <u>Half Serious</u>.

So here's what happens, in translation:

I start by talking about the weather. Either there is a lot of precipitation due to the rainy season or a typhoon. I talk vaguely about humidity coming from one of these causes.

Now I'm going into unknown vocabulary territory. Although I do know the words mould and clothing, I don't know the words for closet or drawers.

I also know the words for box and small round white things.

Unfortunately, I don't know how to tie all the known words together in such a way that a clerk in a store can instantly understand and help me.

I try to use the words I know in a very disjointed fashion, illustrating clothing by touching what I'm wearing and holding my hands in the shape and size of the box I seek.

Since this is Nippon, I'm not shewed away with a shake of the head; not abandoned and left standing alone by a fleeing clerk; subjected to eye-rolling or mocking laughter;

or lashed out at with harsh words about my linguistic incompetence and non-local origins.

I'm almost certain that all of those reactions would be dumped upon a non-anglophone trying to communicate in my poor way in an anglophone milieu.

I already do experience those types of reactions, as an anglophone among anglophones, when I'm having difficulty making a request or understanding something.

Non-anglophones are always much kinder, more patient, and more generous with me when I stumble in another language.

During my quest for a box in Nippon, when I try to communicate with different clerks in different stores they display a number of different sympathetic and kind facial expressions, the most common being puzzlement and an apologetic look for not understanding my gibberish.

Sometimes it's as if the clerks feel badly for not being able to decode my clearly unclear and incomprehensible, and thus secret message to them.

As a language learner I know how to ask questions in a roundabout way when I don't know the name of something.

In Japanese, I start by apologizing because I don't know the word to describe what I am looking for in the store.

Then I start with the weather because I can talk about it with some fluency thanks to hearing the same vocabulary for years in weather reports here and repeating what I hear.

I hope that writing this item will help me to remember the only word that I really need to know and put in a simple sentence: shikketori.

It's sold in packages of three. They are three plastic boxes.

Each one contains mostly liquid with a moisture-absorbing liquid chemical in the shape of small white orbs floating on top of the chemical.

The orbs absorb moisture from the air and dissolve into the liquid. When all the orbs disappear, there is only liquid remaining in a box.

Then the box has to be replaced with a new one.

It's so simple and yet so difficult to describe without the word shikketori.

When the clerks I confront finally realize what I mean and take me to the row of merchandise where shikketori is displayed, both the clerk and I share very broad happy smiles.

I thank each clerk profusely and apologetically, congratulating her on being able to understand what I'm trying to find in the store.

Mariko says that the clerks who I encounter in this manner must go home and talk to their family and friends about the strange non-local who asks them how to find something with a name he doesn't know.

I ask the clerk to tell me the word I don't know, but forget it because I normally only need to buy this product once every six months.

Unused vocabulary drifts away.

But when I finally do remember "shikketori", I'll no doubt wonder why one brand of this product uses a cartoon image of an elephant instead of a bird. Birds like me forget?

### Adding confusion

On other occasions I have more difficulty and a clerk requires much more patience, when I try to buy a box of blueberry-flavoured vinegar drink.

I think that I know the right word because of my first days in Nippon at age 19. Then, I buy little red boxes of algae that is flavoured with vinegar and sugar.

It looks like sticks of chewing gum but tastes much better and is probably healthier too. It's called su kombu, but I mislearn it as sui kombu.

So when I try to tell the clerk that I'm looking for a the vinegar drink I say "sui" kombu drink without the kombu.

Of course she takes me to the kombu first, no doubt puzzled by the idea of drinking it.

She tries to tell me that I might be looking for su instead of sui, but to no avail. I don't realize she's correcting me.

She tries to help me by saying su kombu and takes me to where it's selling.

Despite her patience, I'm getting the impression that I should let her go back to her work. I'm only creating stress for her by frustrating all her efforts to help me.

She's not my personal guide in the store. But as we walk aimlessly past various rows of groceries, I finally spot the vinegar section and see what I want to buy.

I excitedly point it out to her and ask her to pronounce the word su for me. It's an easy word to remember, if you know it in the first place. I thank her very apologetically.

Even a simpler product purchase is more complicated for my incomprehensible self. All I want to buy is laundry detergent for a clothes washer.

For years, I simply find the detergent powder in super-markets. But when I'm seeking the lowest price in a larger, unfamiliar store, things get complicated.

I use pantomime, with varying results.

An older clerk soon takes me to the laundry detergent aisle after I say that clothing gets dirty and rub my shirt as if trying to clean it, saying that I need something for this task.

Another day I get very puzzled looks from a younger clerk before she understands and takes me to the appropriate aisle.

In her case, I repeat the previous day's pantomime, then have to point at bars of soap and indicate that I can use them for my hands, but I need something different to wash my shirt and pants.

I run out of pantomime and explanations. Fortunately, the bars of soap visual aid gets me to the laundry detergent.

## Languicide?

As I say to my cousin Kaeren:

Although I study Latin for two years in secondary school, I forget most of it because I never encounter native speakers or language learners who will speak with me in Latin.

If Latin speakers don't talk to others, Latin will surely be a dead language soon after Rome's empire is no more.

Or it will be corrupted and broken into randomly pronounced sounds and grammatically weird parlance or converted into other tongues.

That's happening to English today.

Broadcasting and anglophiles and anglophones with "more advanced" formal education are already dismembering and extinguishing English.

## Illiterati

Formerly, illiterate means someone unable to read or write due to lack of formal schooling. Now it means the opposite.

Are proletariat and ant-illiterati alike or opposites? How about antiletariat?

No littering.

## Brushes with confusion

Another linguistic problem I have is confusing words in one language or two. Mariko sometimes does so too.

When I say "thing" in Japanese, she hears "monkey" in Español.

While describing a half price store announcement that I hear in Japanese to Mariko, I inadvertently change the word to toothpaste.

I'm not talking about a half price toothpaste sale.

Some linguistic confusion can become rude or offensive. We warn our students about it.

We can only imagine what they'll think when they hear Hispanohablantes talking about eating "vaca con ajo". In Buenos Aires, I make Yumi laugh by saying I'm "un chiko".

### Obese language

Mariko tells the story of another student learning French in Québec City during her studies there. The student speaks Japanese as a first language, i.e. she's Japonophone?

During French class the instructor uses the words débu and important.

The Japonophone student thinks that the instructor is saying she's fat.

Knowing several languages makes this type of linguistic confusion more probable. It gets even more complicated if you deliberately confuse languages, for humour.

Mariko and I jokingly pronounce the letter "J" as if we're speaking Español, when we're talking about all people and places with names starting with a "J".

We become so accustomed to joking this way that we both have to consciously make sure to pronounce the "J" when we refer to the name of a subway station in Fukuoka.

If I take a bus to the station, I always have to make sure that I'm asking the driver if he's going to Jiromaru Station instead of Hiromaru Station.

Mariko has to do the same thing when she gives a student the instructions for going to that station.

The letter "J" brings up an interesting question.

A very popular Spanish-speaking U.S. singer and actor is named Jennifer.  So people should called her Hennifer, right?

### Jaspañol: chewable?

Tegami translates as hand paper in English.  Digami involves no hand or paper.

### Nishi branches out

Nishi phones to ask Mariko if he can cut branches off the plum tree so that he can do his work at Tenjin North.

I understand the question, sort of, and Mariko already tells him it's okay to cut branches.

I know the words for plum and tree in Japanese, but I don't know the word for branches.  So I say the plum tree fingers. Somehow he understands, from the context.

To make sure that I'm not authorizing him to cut down the whole tree, I send Nishi an e-mail message.

To do so I have to find the Japanese word for branch. Looking up plum tree branch at an internet website only nets me translations of each word separately.

So I use the kanji for branch and attach a stock picture of a plum tree branch with a bird on it. It's an artist's rendering. Nishi writes back saying that he understands.

Mariko later confirms that Nishi and I actually do communicate effectively. All we have in common is our human communication skills, not linguistic fluency.

## Treed hardly

Woods have necks, heads, and can operate motor vehicles so well that they secure chauffeurs' jobs.

## Commonalities

Common human characteristics include a skeletal structure, internal organs, limbs, ears, noses, eyes, mouths, etc. Common sense isn't.

## Disclosure

From the outset, the gardener sees only green. He plants flower seeds, only afterwards deciding to use an enclosure to protect the growing flowers by using a line of shrubs.

So he sets aside some money regularly to buy them.

Later on he concludes that it will take too long to accumulate enough savings this way.

So he decides that the best thing to do is to take his funds to the race track and place wagers on every horse running.

Unfortunately this depletes his savings. His loses exceed his gains.

In the end he has no enclosure and loses all his savings.

Moral: Don't put money into a line.

(Mariko gets the gist of this humorous riddle-like story, but says it may be too obscure to be understood. I tell her that a clowning student at Carleton University credits me with making "intellectual" jokes.)

### You have your nerve

You can be nervous or unnerved. In the first case you can involve others and in the second you lose your own. It's better to keep it to yourself.

When I say something humorously insulting to my Granny Mary, she often says, "I like your nerve!" I wonder which one she means.

### Redesigning a breeze

Can wind be repaired? Can we make a less fragile variety?

### Properties

Inappropriate behaviour includes eating, sleeping, dressing casually, and wearing a sweater if needed.

Less well-known is outappropriate behaviour, which can be indistinguishable from inappropriate behaviour and also go beyond it in other respects.

You can appropriate both behaviours anywhere you wish.

# Small joke

The letters "ko" are added to the end of names and words to indicate either child, or enthusiasm, or need.

So women of Mariko's generation and before end up with "ko" behind their names reflecting the long dominance of male supremism religionism.

In the sense of enthusiasm or need, a person who loves to watch television is described as a terebiko.

Likewise, a child with two parents working outside the home can be called a kagiko because s/he needs to carry a house key to get in the door of his/her home.

Using "ko" as a diminutive form also exists, but I only hear it in humorous ways. Usually I'm the one being funny, sometimes accidentally, by adding "ko" to words where it doesn't belong.

The best example is saying that because I love to eat mochi, I'm either a mochiko or komochi. This is a popular joke among people I talk to in Nippon.

But the implications of "ko" also give me some funny ideas beyond that variety. I apply the "ko" sound implications to English words.

Thus a commotion becomes a small one. In football, a collateral avoids a fumble. Beyond football it could be a small down payment that goes sideways.

A co-conspirator is only marginal. A coincidence is a less significant one? When two surgeons work together it's cooperation for each?

Coma is a small mother or a top made in Nippon?

Coefficient indicates mostly not? A coalition is inherently weak? A co-founder is minor? A cog is not capitalized? A co-habitant gets a short-term lease?

A correspondent would be a laconic communicator or a short emergency worker.

A colleague is bantam or the like.

A connotation is short-hand or passing reference? A cos-ponsor is not a major donor.

A collie seems to be a pun referring to frankness and/or Chinese origins. A collapse is a temporary or minor bout with dementia?

To my knowledge, a correction is outside my personal experience. Ask someone who would know.

### Coup?

"Ah! Mon cou!" is a Japanese complaint not endemic to Nippon.

### Censorship

It's an empty vessel or one carrying a secret cargo.

### Equestrian question

Horses often give the impression that they are conservatives of the negative variety.

# Not working?

It's another aspect of the concept that observing behaviour changes it.

An employer who observes its employeed changes how they behave in a manner that either doesn't please them or doesn't please the employer.

"Efficiency experts" should know this fact. Do they?

Employers always effectively criticize their employeed for not devoting enough time and energy and not showing enough enthusiasm toward the role that the employers decide for, dictate to, and expect of the employeed.

Part of this critique is to say that work expands to fill the time available.

At the same time, scientists conclude that moving at the speed of light slows time.

I wonder if the corollary is equally valid, i.e. immobility speeds up time. Thus the inactive have shorter lives? In terms of the effects of sedentary living on health, yes.

In employment terms, working more has the effect of slowing time, which increases "productivity" regardless of the employeeds' reluctance to serve only the interests of the employer?

Yet some employeed tell me that "keeping busy" accelerates the passage of time. So "keeping busy" decreases productivity?

Remaining unmoved by the employers' interests and consequently not doing more work in less time speeds up time and thus enables the employed to go home more quickly?

Non-"productivity" is a good approach for the employed.

The perspectives of employers and scientists are incompatible.

But then again, time is artificial. It only exists in our minds.

The only purpose that humanity-blind employers are capable of recognizing for the employeed's very existence is to increase the employers' monetary and material gains at any and all cost to the employeed and their lives.

If the employeed do not serve their purpose as defined by the employer, the employeed have no purpose or meaning. There is no justification for the employeeds' lives.

The employed are of no value. They are worthless, irrelevant, and expendable. Every employeed person can be replaced. Every job can be eliminated.

The employed are no more than, as Charles Dickens' Ebeneezer Scrooge puts it, "the surplus population". They are terminated when their service is no longer required.

Employers describe this inegalitarian, dictatorial relationship by using the word "productivity" as a euphemism.

Advancing robotic technologies obediently serve the interests of the employers alone, without question, thought, pause, salaries, benefits, or resistance.

Those technologies can help the employer to rid the world of the employeed forever.

### Captivating world

When humans are held by a cell with four bars, they aren't sapiens. Their minds are captivated by captivity.

All the inanity going on behind and in front of bars make the cell a truly PADDed one. (*Personal Advertising Delivery Device)

### Celled parade

The ever-popular, annual parades of people happily and jokingly dressing up like zombies has one missing element to make it more authentic.

Every participant should carry a cell phone. (They probably already do.)

### Having car trouble

In Barcelona (España) the toxic gas spouting, deadly projectiles politely called "cars" are getting a green light to turn right and a flashing amber light to caution that humans are sneaking across car country's "crosswalk".

When humans do have the audacity to enter car country, the only red appearing is in the eyes of enraged motorists seeing an overly bold trespasser on their land.

Maybe the signals are just to indicate that there's game for the cars to hunt.

Drivers completely oblivious to and out of touch with they're spewing tailpipes and their deadly aiming at humanity are behaving like caretaker society children.

Such children hate being disturbed from their unrestricted pursuit of idle fantasies.

Cars are trying to race between humans or grudgingly edging up to rub bumpers on legs.

It's just like one of the last surviving U.K. colonial pale face "masters" who gives me a menacing look as he rubs my legs with his metallic front bumper at a Xiang Giang side street corner. His face says, "Feel lucky punk!"

Most smaller roads and corners have another problem. Cars park bumper-to-bumper so that humans cannot get between them to cross the street.

These vehicles of derangement also block off the only non-road passageways available to humans, areas appropriately called "side" walks.

It's just like far away Gloria, in Rio de Janeiro.

The central, most important area of every street, with the exception of mid-boulevard promenades, is car country.

In great contrast, there aren't usually walkways with "side" roads. A side road is just another car road.

### Shoes instead

For generations, affluent sedentary older people are credited with stimulating the sale of bigger, more expensive models of cars and driving them everywhere.

I buy snowshoes.

### Funny you shouldn't ask or say that...

Don't encourage me or try to discourage me, but...

If there is another volume of humour in my life and head it won't be called <u>The Next Joke Book</u> or <u>A Funny Thing Didn't Happen To Me On The Way To Death</u>.

Some potential titles are <u>Humour Me Senseless</u>, <u>Not Getting The Last Laugh</u>, <u>Nonsense of Humour</u>, <u>Finding Your Sense Of Humour (& Wishing You Hadn't)</u>, <u>Nonsensically,</u> and, <u>Losing You Senseless</u>.

In response to this promise, or threat, some readers may put my identity in question by responding, "Are you Joe King?"

### Seasonal swipes

If there is noël, what is there?

Nowell caused by drought.

It's beginning to look a lot like quishmas, everywhere you cook.

## 好 好 好

A Christmas news story causes Mariko to point out the visible and typical blatant falseness of yet another long unquestioned, unchallenged, and obvious myth.

The north pole is located on Earth's ocean, not on land.

"How can Santa live at the North Pole. There is no land there. It's on the Arctic Ocean." Mariko says.

Only upon hearing these words does the significance of this basic planetary fact finally dawn on me.

I suddenly realize why Chuang Hwa wants to be considered an Arctic country.

Just as Chuang Hwa builds artificial islands in the Pacific to set up military bases nowadays, hundreds of years ago it secretly builds an island in the Arctic Ocean, code name: Santa's Workshop.

This also explains why made-in-Chuang Hwa Santa replicas at the Chinese owned dollar stores look Chinese.

Yes, Santa, the elves, and the reindeer are all Chinese military personnel who have created stealth technology enabling them to invade every home on Earth in a single night.

Rudolph's Red Nose was added during Mao's time. It is a euphemism for a missile top? And how about missile toe? It is a malady of missile inspectors?

Perhaps the clincher is in Santa's own famous and often repeated Chinese words. Evidence comes in the form of the names of two Chinese restaurants.

When I'm a university student, one of my classes frequents the two culinary establishments. I'm too busy studying to go, but my fellow students tell me the telling tale.

They say that one Chinese restaurant is called, "Ho", which they say translates into English as "good". They say the other Chinese restaurant is called, "Ho Ho", which they say translates as "very good".

Thus Santa's Chinese origins are revealed in his very words, Ho! Ho! Ho!

This also makes me wonder about the roots of a certain giant who lives in a valley and whose image is displayed on tins of vegetables.

Green is, after all, one of the colours of Christmas.

These revelations also explain why the Chinese Spring Festival is mistakenly called Chinese New Year and why nobody talks about the corresponding, but here made obvious, Chinese Christmas that is so widely celebrated.

### Unreal card

Shortly before announcing the sale of cyberspace-only trading cards depicting himself as a superhero, Punchline says he wants to be reinstated as emperor without election.

The humour of this false entitlement is irresistible.  It conjures up visions of past phantasms joining the ludicrous claim to power of the ridiculous.

When does "stirring things up", as Punchline's supporters celebrate him with doing, make them unappetizing and too tough to eat bread?

I must recite a list of other defeated candidates, like Punchline, but most deceased, saying they are throwing their support under Punchline, saying they're right behind him.

It's the ideal location for laughing.

However, their largely posthumous support isn't without proviso.

Each supports Punchline's bid to return only on condition that each of them gets to serve full eight year terms first. Only in the thereafter could Punchline be reinstated.

That would be at least 32 years from now, at which time the currently mid-70s year old Punchline could continue his pathological lying by declaring himself still alive.

## Pain

One person's pain is another person's bread. Yet sometimes the two can sound closer, such as when there are problems with électricité or courant.

### "Security" kills painful fear

A researcher at Montréal's McGill University finds that fear deactivates the part of the brain which suppresses pain.

I extrapolate that fear of crime and "terrorism" could make them a greater source of psychological pain.

Since few people have personal encounters with crime and "terrorism", fear of them is an artificially-induced fear that becomes a source of pain.

"Security" measures become a very addictive pain-killer for people who are afraid of something that they never experience personally.

"Security" measures thus assure that a person who fears will feel no pain, like a drunk?

## Hail security?

Remembering an old cartoon that I see on television as a child, a cartoon drawn up and filmed for my parents' generation during their early adulthood, I rewrite it.

I mean I rewrite the lyrics to its music. I think that the title is "Der Fuhrer's Face". Here's my rewrite of the words to bring it up to date for the jailkeeper society:

### Insecurity's face

♫umpah umpahpah, umpah um♫

When security says, "Wipe smiles right off your face!"
We stare, stare, like zombies in a trance.
For to joke at security is a big mistake.
So we stare, stare, at insecurity's face.

## Geese that don't fly

I know a couple of Guys. Both live in the Montréal area. One is slim and the other is hefty and athletic. Guys come in many sizes.

Mariko wears one for Aikido practice. She has several so that she'll always have a clean one that's clean and dry.

These guys also come in different sizes because her first one is too large. She eventually abandons it.

The smallest guy I know about must be very tiny and it must be used for opening very small portals. It's a ka-guy.

### Food supply chain problem

Navel oranges sink.

### Inedible & unappetizing

Warning: Due to the chocking hazard and internal organ damage, it is inadvisable to use window dressing.

Some shopping does involve the physical homonym of pain but is otherwise more economical than actually purchasing anything.

The noteable exception is purchasing a product that is an actual transparent wall hole covering.

Windows are normally hard, even if they contain soft ware. But those containing such wares are always opaque and too often annoying.

### Out on a limb

All arms are offensive.

### Pronounciation

People are pronounced in only two ways: married and dead. The spelling gives no hint of these pronunciations.

Silence can require repairs or it can act as a colon, coma, period, apostrophe, semi-colon, etc.

### Not the end all

A prelude could be civil, polite, suggestive, and/or provide a warning.

A prologue is clear cut, whereas an epilogue is likely to be multi-ringed.

A b-log is to writing what a b-film is to cinema?

Latitude and position determine foreshadowing, with no apparent aft.

Stories about mountaineering require a climax. This particular semantic use could indicate a pierced lobe.

Opposition to such expeditions are expressed as anti-climax.

Aftermath is a different class and need not be specified to define the word.

### Escalator out of order

Ukraine' war president invites N.A.T.O. to send all sort of weaponry to fight off Russian advances, assuring the world that the Russian Federation will surrender and withdraw its forces.

So there will be no risk of triggering a world war and nuclear holocaust.

Deutschland declines the Ukrainian president's invitation with two words: No tanks. (But later Deutschland folds like a card player under pressure.)

### Other name changes?

Morgue employees and post-traumatic stress psychiatrists are now called war analysts?

Kidnappers are responsible for giving young goats a rest.

Non-toxic snacks can be called safecrackers.

## Faceless messes

Making use of an airheaded screen all-broadcasting system called "youtube" results in viewing only random items pre-selected and presented in random order, jumping from one unrelated subject or broadcast or segment of a broadcast to another.

The beginning of a broadcast can become the end or be placed somewhere in the middle. Multi-part interviews are presented in randomly-ordered disorder.

An interview can thus continue where it leaves off or conclude before it begins or continues.

It's like flipping open a book and starting to read part of a sentence in the middle of a page and then immediately switching to another page and reading only the beginning of a sentence. The writing is never going to be understood.

To paraphrase an expression: Give enough monkeys enough words and they will see the same number of words as all the words in some famous or unknown writer's works.

Commercials are inserted randomly, interrupting speakers, interviews, and discussions in mid-sentence, making them disjointed and more difficult to understand by breaking their chain of thought and distracting viewers from the reasoning and logic underpinning and supporting the speaker's words. Whatever is intended becomes jibberish.

The resulting, meaningless airhead mishmash is based entirely on "tracking" data and "algorithms", not getting to know, carefully observing, and patiently interviewing actual living viewers and learning the bases upon which they plan, schedule, and make their deliberate and well-thought-out choices or their actual interests or viewing behaviours.

Maybe the viewer is only like a bored TV watcher who is "channel surfing" to find something interesting. So the data collected on his/her "surfing" is entirely meaningless.

The mishmash resulting is less than a guess. It's a gross generalization gone rampant. It becomes no more than automatically dictating what viewers see and when.

It's an airhead dictatorship model that can only render all viewers very confused, senseless, and completely dis-oriented victims of attention span deficiency.

### Teaching humans tricks

Having learned how to touch a screen to receive food, such as a pizza delivery, humans are becoming adept at immitating the behaviour of higher forms of life, such as monkeys.

The latest advance in this regard is reported by U.S. CBS News.

According to that source, a human music composer is now listening intently to bird songs and transcribing them into sheet music of human musical notes and compositions.

This means that humans are now becoming almost as good at imitating sounds that they don't understand as another higher form of life, the budgie, the cockatoo, or at least the macaws. Wow!

Perhaps, eventually, over millions of years, humans might evolve into a higher form of life too, one that is capable of understanding and communicating with every form of terrestrial life on this planet.

And who knows, humans might eventually evolve in intelligence to the point of attracting the attention of superior extraterrestrial beings who will adopt human animals as their best friend house pets.

Hey-hey! Human want a cracker! Human want a touch screen!

## Suite your...

The work of a tailor and a seamstress is always so-so?

## News?

All news isn't good or bad. Sometimes it's like a horse without means. Other times it can sound like an outmoded instrument of capital punishment or a leg movement.

## Tour guide

A tour of duty is a nightmarish short visit to death, destruction, maiming, trauma, deprivation, and loss producing violent memories which endure an indeterminate length of time, if not an entire lifetime.

The experience can be passed on through later generations by vivid stories, violent abuse, and dependency on human or chemical support.

### Churnman

Einstein is a mug?  Oppenheimer is an open house?

### Hearty

Halfhearted is better or worse than a full one or none at all?

### Hoarse shoo

Gah! Gah!

### Elder abuse

When I'm a small child, my maternal grandma abuses one of her adult daughters, my aunt.

Every time that my aunt and uncle plan to go on vacation, grandma falls ill and they cancel their trip.

This happens so many times that grandma has no credibility in everyone's eyes.  But my aunt and uncle never get away.

Grandma goes through the same routine every time, groaning and moaning as if she's in extreme pain.  It's not pleasant to witness, but it's also strangely funny.

One day I go to visit grandma after school and decide to teach her what I learn from her.  I lie down on her front porch groaning and moaning in her manner.

She comes to the door and behaves as if she's truly concerned, asking me frantically what's wrong with me.  I get up and laugh, telling her it's just a joke.

Then she starts her groaning and moaning in the same way. She thinks I'll fall for this act?  I ask her if she's all right and then add a question.

"I was just wondering if you are leaving me something in your will?"  She suddenly stops her act.  It's a miracle!?

In the end she leaves me nothing except the memory of her elder abuse antics.  It's a lesson in melodrama.

She leaves her adult children with the money that they give her to help her out.  Instead of spending it, she puts it in the bank as "their inheritance".

Is this a joke too or a pioneering example of tax free savings wherein the heirs pay the provincial government a probate percentage fee on their own money?

### Royal T

So many monarchs are dead.  The butterfly is endangered.

William Lyon Mackenzie King is buried.  Elvis The King is also long dead, as is Nat King Cole.  So are Martin Luther King I and II.  Gabrielle Roy also departed.

Earl Cameron is gone.  Duke Ellington is gone.  Prince is deceased.  So is The Queen of Rock'n'Roll, Tina Turner.

"The King of Kensington" signs off years before them.

The only survivors are Martin Luther King III, Stephen King, Queen Latifa, and Lady Gaga.

## Abilities

People can be able and unable. Can they be disembodied at the same time?

## Appointments

Those who are appointed and who are not appointed can both be disappointed.

## On the trail

Trailers accompany and follow pseudo-campers and film-makers.

## Shelling

Clams are credited with being positively emotional and, unlike humans, can both ascend and descend without uttering a word.

## Same tuberon

Shark infestations are oceanic, poolemic, cardographic, speculative, and greedy.

## Disunited Queen dome

Europe's U.K. island nation-state uses the letters U.K. to describe itself. In long form the European country is the United Kingdom of Great Britain and Northern Ireland.

It's the most cumbersome nation-state name that I know of, so the abbreviation makes sense. There is some misunderstanding of the word "Great".

It's like the old Greater Vancouver Regional District. The word great and greater simply refers to an area. It is not a statement or implication of grandeur or vastness.

In terms of current politics, the most accurate long name for the U.K. would be the Disunited Kingdom of some parts of Scotland with England and Wales, and part of Northern Ireland.

But this is too realistic and accurate for the self-repressive, emotionally-self-constraining, except in war and argument, U.K. English literature image of the typical U.K.er elite.

So I suggest a minor but major change in name to reflect the monarchical dictatorship heritage reflected in the abbreviation U.K.

Since the longest reigning U.K. monarchs are female not male, i.e. queens, not kings, I suggest that the nation-state change its name to the U.Q. or United Queendom.

This would also be a great statement in favour of sexual equality and LGBTQ people in the U.Q.

I send this idea to a U.K. monarchy website, <u>The Times of London</u> newspaper, and the U.K. prime minister. Will they not be amused? I get no replies.

### Commemorating pandemic?

COVID-19 also goes by the name Corona, which is the name of a Toyota car and a brand of beer.

The U.K. must have plans to commemorate the beginning of the fourth year of the world pandemic. That nation-state is having a Corona shun.

## Cold discomfort

A past government study of the Canadian immigrant experience reveals that it can be ten years before a newcomer is invited into the home of anyone born in Canada.

Yes, life can be cold in Canada. It's difficult to avoid an icy reception. There's no skating around it. And breaking the ice can be perilous. No one wants to be left on thin ice.

If you must, remain guarded with a small red and white boat.

Take refuge by burrowing, but avoid another form of borough, especially if a polar bear is riding atop.

## Sick society: news drug culture

For many years, U.S. network evening news programmes are dominated by commercials from big pharmaceutical companies offering medications for all ailments.

Taken together, they represent a snake oil cure-all for every ailment known or imaginable, including so many that I've never heard of before seeing the commercials.

The commercials don't encourage viewers to take care of themselves as preventative medicine, by adopting healthy lifestyles, diets, and regular exercise.

Instead, the commercials offer symptom-hiding or repression and/or pain-killing laboratory concoctions to people who may or may not already be ill.

This reminds me of morning after birth control pills or driving recklessly because injuries can be repaired by doctors.

Just take a pill and you'll feel better or forget that you're sick. Maybe you'll get better too. Either way there's no need to change your way of life. Buy our product.

Hmm. Maybe they should sell pills causing memory loss.

That way, commercial audiences can forget what might be wrong, take a pill, and forget how much it costs to purchase it. This can also head off law suits for side effects.

Drug commercials list symptoms that might indicate a person has the specific sickness that an advertised pharamaceutical product is supposed to help or hide, and also advises viewers to "Ask your doctor."

It's as if doctors aren't taking care of their patients and not examining them thoroughly. The commercial implies that "your doctor" doesn't know you're sick. Tell your doctor.

While all this "information" is being conveyed by voice and large letters, the bottom of the screen shows warnings that pharmaceutical companies must legally describe.

Reading the small print is essential. During such commercials, I turn off the screen volume and don't read the large letters.

So I have no idea what ailments are targeted.

Ignoring the pharmaceutical companies main messages, I take a close look at the small print warnings. Anyone doing the same would be likely to avoid the product altogether.

For even a single product, I read so many side effects warnings that I conclude the cure is worse than the ailment.

In very small print, pharmaceutical companies' commercials list side effects such as: shortness of breath, diarrhea, fainting, vomiting, abdominal pain, hives, constipation, indigestion, dizziness, rash, swelling of tongue, lips, & mouth; cancer, stroke, heart attack, and death. Some cure!

So when I see a story in the U.S. news about the healthy effects of doing yoga, such as relaxing the body, lowering stress, and reducing certain health risks, a scenario arises.

Some U.S.er watching all the medication commercials may passively notice the news about the healthy effects of yoga and decide to go to a pharmacy to ask questions.

The U.S.er will ask the pharmacist if there are any yoga pills in stock.

### Propaganda nomenclature

Dominant empires change throughout history, from Mongols to Romans to Portuguese, to Spanish, to French, to U.K. to C.C.C.P. and to U.S.

Now Chuang Hwa and Bharat are re-emerging and Russia is coming back to life as "capitalist" nation-states which the U.S., E.U., and associate nation-states call adversaries.

A very moneyed person in the associate nation-states is called a billionaire, but if s/he is Russian s/he is an "oligarch". In real life, all billionaires are oligarchs.

But the "adversary" has to have a negative and villainous-sounding label, even if all billionaires are greedy hoarders who have no qualms about their surplus and few if any concerns about the well-being of the vast majority of people.

Even more bizarre are the distinctions made between "capitalist" business people in Bharat and Chuang Hwa.

If these moneyed people are in Bharat they're called millionaires or billionaires, as their counterparts are in the associate nation-states.

But if they are in Chuang Hwa they are derided as "communists". What is a billionaire oligarch communist?

This is the bogus nomenclature made up by falling imperial orders that cannot compete with the "newcomer upstarts" as opposed to the highly competitive capitalist start-ups that they are in reality.

### Added new title

The latest etiquette of expertise being added to my vocabulary of the bizarre is "retirement coach". This is a retired person spreading his/her expertise?

Or is it someone forming sports teams composed of retired people? Or the team is called "Retirement"?

The "retirement coach" I see interviewed in the news appears to be too young to be retired. So this person is a not-confined-to-an-armchair coach?

Perhaps even more or less interesting is a news report of complaints about tax increases for alcohol following medical research finding that any amount of alcohol consumption is unhealthy.

A news reporter interviews a "beer expert".

Shouldn't this expertise be categorized and explained? Such an expert could be merely tipsy, drunk, drunkard, alcoholic, sick, or – top category: dead.

"Data ethicist" puzzles me. Which part is the actual adjective? Under what circumstances and by what means is the ethical conduct of data determined?

How can an inanimate entity have or not have ethics? What type of training is required to be an ethicist of data?

### Highest ranking

As I start saying when I'm at university: Every generalization, without exception, is completely false.

### Magalopolis

Former U.S. Emperor Twit Punchline is seeking vengeance for his decisive electoral defeat by depicting himself as the one who is the voice of "most people" and the one who will exact "retribution" for wrongly-done-by "most people".

He promises to do so by going after his successful opponents and non-supporters.

I don't understand.

How can "most people" relate to or support anyone like Punchline, who is born into privilege and money and who is a party to acts making "most people" wrongly-done-by and who thus falsely claims to be their voice?

How can "most people" reject, decry, and rally against U.S. Presiden Biden, i.e. someone who, much like themselves, is born into a humble family with only adequate means and who thus knows his fellow "most people" very well?

The meaning of Punchline's slogan letters needs to be rewritten to make them silly, unpalatable, and embarrassing for his very base and fanatical churchist fundamentalist extremist supporters to use.

I come up with a few possibilities and credit them to words composed of the initials of his actual slogan. They are:

My Aunt Gets Arthritis; Machineguns And Gangs Alliance; Make Anti-Christ Govern Again; My Almighty God Assaulter; Morons Against Good Acts; Might Actually Get Arrested; Millions Afraid General Alert; Makeup Anything Get Attention; Many Agree Gays Attractive; Malicious Agitators Go Atrocious; Mindless Assailants Goad All; Megalomaniac Aggressor's Greed Awful; Mock And Goad All; Maim And Gut Attacker; Millions Are Getting Afflicted; Megalomaniac Agitates Gullible Audience; etc.

Signed, Delirious Jester Trap; Dilettante Jokes Terribly; etc.

### Newseum add from NHK World

Title displayed under television news story, all caps:

CHINESE FOREIGN MINISTRY
WARNS US OVER TAIWAN

# Inanimate animating

Sometimes I don't believe my own ears, particularly when I hear a "news reader" saying things like this: "Documents were forced to be revealed." What can that mean?

Yes, as Mariko notices, I have a knack for figuring out incomprehensible phrases coming from the mouths of overconfident pseudo-second-language speakers.

But how can a document be forced and what is the connection between that and the words "to be revealed"?

I can hardly imagine how any "thing" can be forced to be revealed. I only understand the concept of forcing open a door because it fits too tightly in its frame.

I could go for someone being forced to reveal him/herself, as being an imposter or a spy. But how can something inanimate be forced "to be revealed"?

Of course documents can be exposed, to sunlight and rain, etc. Then they can be said to be exposed to the elements.

After this encounter with the incomprehensible, Mariko tells me that a non-fluent anglophile tells her that she can only use the word "degree" for temperature.

Does this mean I have to return my degrees to campus? Or are they hot documents that I have to surrender to the police?

Mariko and I are forever surprised by the degree of ignorance that's attempting to pass itself off as absolute knowledge.

The less you learn, the more you believe you know.

### Bird cooking?

An anglophone Al Jazeera news reporter with a U.K. accent says, "The U.S. is pressurizing Turkeye."

Is this a reference to some recipe using the former and apparently incorrect English katakana pronunciation of the nation-state's name?

Or is the U.S. training Turkeye for some deep sea diving adventure?

### And now a message for all of the worriers, negativists, and pessimists:

As the old songs lyrics say, "Enjoy yourself, it's later than you think"; and, "get happy and get ready for the judgement day..."

When Mariko tells me about friends of friends whose spirits are going down and down into an abyss, I suggest conveying this message to them:

The nation-states' huge nuclear stockpiles accumulated by the U.S., N.A.T.O., Chuang Hwa, Russian Federation, etc. Increase the likelihood of a nuclear holocaust that destroys all humans and most other life on earth.

Such a conflict would mean that everyone would be dead. So there's nothing to worry about. Just enjoy your life while you still can.

I remind Mariko that when I set out on my brief introductory exploration of the southern Americas, people in the news are very worried too.

Then, they're worried that la guerra de las Malvinas between a collapsing U.K. government and Argentina's collapsing military dictatorship of the time could lead to a world war, i.e. a nuclear holocaust because the U.K. belongs to N.A.T.O. and the C.C.C.P. provides assistance to the dictators.

But I boarded my flight to Buenos Aires, saying that if there were a nuclear war it would be better to be vapourized at an epicentre than to be far away and suffer indefinitely from prolonged radiation sickness and all the pain and suffering entailed.

Why prolong the agony?  Get it over with quick and fast.

### National insecurity threats

The greatest threats facing the U.S. during my first months in Winnipeg are balloons and internet dancers.

There are about 300 balloons flying over the U.S. at the time and, like all airline passengers or all ages, every one is considered a potentially dangerous suspect.

We are all now guilty until proven innocent and we are all getting a taste of how the least moneyed and least advantaged people are routinely treated by bureaucrats.

The increasingly hyper-paranoid and afraid of strong competition U.S.A. now declares balloons to be mystery objects which are undoubtedly spying for Chuang Hwa.

There is no concrete evidence to support the deranged-sounding allegations, which are mindlessly parroted by people claiming to be objective and intelligent journalists.

But convincing itself, like a person who religiously believes his/her own self-deluding illusions, the U.S. sends war planes to shoot down balloons flying near and over it.

One is shot down over the ocean. Another is shot down over the Arctic. That one is too difficult to find and examine to see whether or not it's a "spy" balloon.

Destroyed pieces of the one shot down over the ocean are recovered, but there is no word on exactly what it is or was. There are vague reports about it "probably spying".

But nobody is offering actual proof. It must be kept secret so that no one outside the military will know that the balloon is only for scientific research.

That side of the story leaks out when a scientist outside the military makes a comment about balloons in the air.

In defiance of reality and in deference to face-saving, the 300 balloons and scientific research don't get the same lengthy news coverage as the "spy balloon" shoot-down.

Reporters and the officials that they interview keep using the term "spy balloon" as if nothing happened and the balloons justify new military spending and distrust of Chuang Hwa.

Dancers on the internet are a threat for different reasons.

They're using a software application owned by a company in Chuang Hwa instead of one owned in the U.S. and its associate states.

The software is used mostly by teenagers, mainly female, and the advertisers and politicians who want to attract their patronage.

The software is just like the ones owned in the U.S. and associate states, in terms of personal data collected and used for business purposes.

But it's unacceptable and threatening for capitalist Chuang Hwa to do the same as the U.S. and associate states and to do it better and attract more followers.

### Blanketing (covering up abuses)

I write about the latest excuse words for abusing people and denying them choices in life. The currently most famous ones are "for security reasons", "due to rising oil prices", etc.

But I neglect to mention perhaps the oldest and perhaps most frequently used excuse: "in today's world".

I hear this one from childhood, although this blanket excuse for making life more difficult than necessary no doubt dates back far before my childhood.

This excuse or some variation of it would be used during the eras of "highway robbery" in Europe and or "stage coach bandits" by U.S.ers of European descent.

This excuse would also be useful for criminalizing all people who opposed monarchical dictatorship. "In today's world we have to watch out for "democracy insurgents".

## Spelling it out telephonically

The difficulty of communicating the correct spelling through a telephone is a classic example of the importance of the encoder and decoder of messages.

In an attempt to reduce misunderstanding, many decoders use a U.S.-military-based system.

It goes something like this: C as in Charlie, A as in Apple, or Alpha, B as in Beta, N as in Nancy, etc.

As a protest against the militarization of spelling and out of sheer mischief and an irresistible urge to mock this particular convention, I become spontaneous in phone spelling.

One of my favourites is E as in elephant. Some decoders actually have a sense of humour, repeat my E with a happy, amused voice, and adopt elephant when confirming decode.

I just make it up as I go along. Aside from elephant, I say whatever word pops into my head when I want to communicate a letter in a word or name I'm spelling.

I have yet to try R as in Rumpelstiltskin, Rapunzel, or radiometre. Nor do I use O as in oligarch. I am more likely to say K as in kaleidoscope, How about T as in topsy turvy or O as in oopsidaisy?

To confuse the decoder more, I would say K as in Knife, X as in xylitol or xenon, E as in extraordinary.

I'm likely to say A as in Aarvark. When talking to a health bureaucrat I might say V as in Vaccination. I haven't used M as in Malpractice yet.

This gets me thinking that there could be a wide variety of categories for people to use while spelling over a telephone.

A stereotypical Irish variety of person might say, L as in Leprechaun, S as in Shillelagh, B as in Blarney, M as in Malarkey, J as in Jig, R as in Riverdance, D as in Donny-brook, E as in Eire, K as in Killarney, G as in Guinness, etc.

If calling from Wales, please say L as in Llanfairpwllgwy-ngyllgogerychwyrndrobwllllantysiliogogogoch.

If calling from New Zealand, please say: T as in Taumata-whakatangihangakoauauotamateaturipukakapikimaungahor onukupokaiwhenuakitanatahu.

The key to telephonically spelling out words and names is to pronounce the actual letters very slowing and clearly, exaggerating the letter's sound.

But if the objective is to add to the confusion, here are some categories that will be useless and unhelpful to the decoders.

In the illiterate category would fall spelling explanations such as E as in illiterate, G as in gnome, P as in phlem, N as in entity and encephalitis, R as in 'rithmetic and 'riting.

The obstinately and snotty intellectual might say A as in autocratic, I as in irascible, O as in obfuscate, X as in xenophobic, L as in lackadaisical, B as in belligerent, M as in monotheism, N as in nepotism, P as in psychiatrist, philanthropist, or philosophy etc. Hm. I might try some of those too.

For people considering themselves a set apart, rather than only the opposite of amateurs, there can be specialized lists, such as: A as in autopsy, A as in anaesthetic, J as in juris-prudence, B as in barrister, C as in cranium, A as in abrasion or autism, T as in theft, R as in rigamortis, I as in investigator, B as in bailiff, R as in recognizance or reconnaisance, H as in honorarium, O as in omnipotent, T as in tetrahedron or trapezoid, etc.

To be obnoxious, a person could say O as in obnoxious, A as in annoying, S as in silly, W as in wasting my time, I as in I want to talk to someone else, C as in Could I speak with your supervisor?

Mariko, the devoted linguist will only use letters that are pronounced the same way as their spoken sound at the beginning of words used for spelling on the phone.

This would include A as in Abraham, not Apple, B as in Beatrice, C as in Cesaer, etc.

### No swimming

You can't go swimming in a donnybrook.

There's something fishy about getting along swimmingly.

Dippers come in all shapes and sizes, but none are called obese.

Swimmers go shopping to get soup ladles?

Swimmers dress formally, masquerade, or wear luggage.

Swimmers don't get out of the swim of things.

Osaka swimmers are speaking dialect when they say Okini, or is that Irish?

A jumping-off a plank isn't interesting?  But it's just the start.

Divers are diverse.  They enter for both liquids and solids. Many dress formally.

Tsukuba suits are found near Tokyo, even during a drought.

Swimmers must have very unhealthy lifestyles and diets. Look what happens every time they get into the water. How do they survive?

Cats love swimmers.  They're perfect.

Swimmers change nationalities, imitate babies and pets, obsess on their navels, and feign death.

### Bricks

People using this building material are either a combination of several nation-states, very strong, or likely to experience pain in their work.

### Impair (useful fruit)

The uses of pair include chute, pluie, sol, rot, scope, and docks.  It's also am in an AC.

## Fruitless rules

If today's nation-state plant and seed import restrictions were in effect when the European invasions of the world began, there would be no tomatoes in Italia's food, no potatoes in Ireland, and no vodka in Russia.

## "Required" lies

Every time that a government/corportate bureaucratic form says that a phone number is "required" we must lie to complete the form because we have no phone.

Every time that a government/corporate bureaucratic form demands that Mariko and I provide our "permanent home address" we have to lie because neither of us has one.

Our parents move us around and we subsequently move ourselves around.

Now that our parents are deceased, we cannot honestly say that we have a "permanent home address".

Bureaucracy seems to imagine that we are all living in the pre-industrial age villages housing generations of our kin and from which none of us will ever move.

This conjures up visions of inbreeding and morons. Is that the genetic lineage from which bureaucrats originate?

## Thoughtlessness

The form letter is a traditional tool used in bureaucratic non-communication. But now a new technology promises/ threatens to produce something even worse.

A "flawless message writer" will soon write everything. It will thus replace the human brain altogether.

Generations of "first" worlders are already not developing handwriting skills because they're learning that they only need to type, not touch-type, with a computer keyboard on a screen.

So future linguistic archaeologists will have to find another Rozetta Stone to decode all the handwritten writings of the world up to now.

As experimental animal hunt-and-peck screen-touching becomes the norm for human animals, and technology becomes the sole author of writing, humans become obsolete.

If none of us write anymore, by any means, none of us will be able to write and we will also become totally illiterate.

So who is going to read the technology's "flawless" messages?

Who reads anything in a completely illiterate world?

Oh! I get it. That's the flaw in the "flawless".

### Easter waker

When someone dies in Nippon, a wake is held. Loved ones sit near the cadaver to verify the death. Mariko says that some people who seem to be deceased revive during wakes.

Applying this reality to one of the religionist stories, perhaps someone who dies and then revives three days later isn't truly dead.

Such a person may be unconscious, perhaps in a coma, and later revives before finally dying.

Or, perhaps the person is the first known zombie.

### Punctuating short stop

The resemblance between coma and comma is more than a single letter difference?  Both involve a pause and one is of indefinite length, as when a speaker pauses to be dramatic or a reader decides to stop reading.

This is a topic which needs to be added to RAMMARG in TJ: JNG?

### Sit down and shut up!

In my schooling, particularly in the elementary years, the most common and frequent instructions coming from the mouths of school teachers are "Sit down and shut up!"

This isn't a precise quote.  The same message is conveyed in various words or in sounds such as SHHHHHHH!

This later perplexes university professors and seminar leaders who become frustrated because first and second year students are taciturn, reluctant to speak or ask questions.

A schooling with silent consequences is typical of my generation.  We're trained not to communicate with others.

Previous generations are told, "Children should be seen, but not heard."

So when older people criticize more recent generations for "lacking social skills", the elders must be joking or suffering from generational memory loss.

The only difference between past and more recent generations is that past generations were silenced, isolated, and separated by humans while more recent generations are trained to end up the same way by inanimate objects, computers.

The computers are gentler and more humane mufflers and muters? They simply mesmerize us into silent stares?

### Getting an ear empty

Generations experience ear drum shattering technology, from loud band concerts in the town square to electric guitars indoors.

Hearing aid manufacturers start with ear horns and eventually produce the tiniest possible hearing aids, ones that are almost invisible.

Is it just a coincidence that private listening electronic devices are so much like the tiny aids, or is the hearing aid industry deliberately increasing its market?

Generations go from big home stereos and portable "ghetto blasters" on their shoulders to simple headsets wired to large and small recording devices to Walkman and disc.

The headsets and devices shrink, some headsets also grow again, with the same purpose: to block out external sounds, such as human voices and oncoming traffic.

A person can walk along a sidewalk and cross a busy road completely unconscious of all around.  At least one person does this along a GO train track once, only once.

Generations go from wearing headsets to listen to private music or messages in complete isolation, to wearing headsets to hear a foggy, confusing, distorted version of reality.

Bluetooth plugs and hearing aids come in the same miniature size and feel the same.  Who can tell the difference in fit?

The listeners' next steps are in silence, as the music fades, all sound waves become inaudible, and the former listeners hear nothing and no one as their world goes silent forever.

Music boxes abound too, and not just the little ones and gigantic ones selling at souvenir stores in Otaru.  In Canada, I literally hear entire motor vehicle music boxes.

Drivers like my Winnipeg friend Frank are wearing hearing aids by the time they reach 50 years of age because they use maximum volume on the loud speakers of music players.

Whenever I hear a driver broadcasting music into the streets in like fashion, often from a vehicle with the windows closed, I call it a "stereo on wheels".

Now that people are broadcasting their "private" mobile telephone conversations into the streets the same way, I can call their passing a "public phone on wheels".

But winter in Winnipeg reveals something far beyond anything that I hear anywhere else.  As I walk through the streets I hear music, not voices, in my head.

I see no source. I only hear it. It's a new mystery for me, until the source approaches and passes me.

People on foot and on bicycles have their music players completely hidden inside their coats and their bicycle bags. It's like a passing concert of unknown origin.

So I have to come up with a name for this phenomenon, based on my previous encounters with mobile music. How about "stereo on foot" and "stereo on peddles"?

## ATMosphere

There are so many "ATM" signs in the urbanscape today that there must be a shortage of molecules.

The conversion of Canada's ABMs to ATMs is disarming acculturation?

## Green Nippon

The Vikings have many colonies, including what becomes Ireland. They found Dublin. Do the Vikings also found Nippon?

What else would explain the widespread use of O in the Japanese language, in prefix, words, expressions, and names, such as O'cha, O'chawan, O'nigiri, O'hio (O'hiyaidesu ne.), O'kamoto, O'hara, O'bayashi, O'nagaishi-masu.

My last word on the subject is O'moshiroi.

Since the annual year end new year celebration in Nippon is called O'shogatsu, it must be an Irish ginger festival, right?

### Collectors

People start collecting things they lack, such as stamps, coins, bottle caps, sea shells, etc.

This explains why nation-states are widely known for trying to collect intelligence.

### Wrongers pro-rights

Historically, as we learn in Newcastle (U.K.), the leading anglophone slave trading nation-state, the U.K., makes a major contribution to ending the European slave trade.

Later, a leading anglophone nation-state that is developed and enriched by slave labour, the U.S., wins its civil war against separatists by officially ending slavery.

Given the decline of democracy in the "west", seen through the historic context of the abolition of the slave trade and slavery, some logical present day conclusions are possible.

Perhaps the Russian Federation and Chuang Hwa will soon become the leading world centres for human rights.

### Universal champions

After nearly 500 years of invasions, destruction, pillaging, theft, bullying, warring, environmental destruction, occupation, illegal settlements, acculturation, genocide, murder, persecution, racism, sexism, discrimination, paedophilia, and other abuses and crimes against humanity around the world, Europeans and their descendents author "The Universal Declaration of Human Rights".

Do as I say, not as I do?  It's an imperial expression.

This final act of the European national-colonial era is like a terrorizing serial killer setting up a "security" company.

I'm writing humour books but the Europeans and their descendants are just kidding, right?

If not, they're taking themselves far too seriously, to the point of extreme self-deception and delirium.

### Life as we don't know it:
### the world beyond bureaucracy

In the completely artificial, contrived, and cloistered world of bureaucracy and its absolute fundamentalist neutrality religionism, the natural world order must be ignored.

If it cannot be ignored, it must be eliminated.

Everything and everyone, animate or inanimate, living or dead, must be defined, redefined, and confined so that it can be fit into tight inflexible rules and forms.

This is the bureaucratic girdle or bustle, i.e. straight jacket. One size fits all.

If the confined don't fit, they must be remoulded to suit bureaucracy.

Deviations and differences are unacceptable and intolerable. All must be folded, affixed, and filed neatly in place by bureaucracy.

Bureaucracy's forms oblige absolute obedience. Bureaucracy unilaterally decides what is "required". No variation or debate is tolerated in bureaucracy's computer forms.

Non-compliance is punishable by law or threat of cancellation and revocation. Making an inaccurate, misleading, or false entry on a form is an offence (to bureaucracy).

In this strange parallel universe of reality-denial, renters and homeless people can only be, bureaucratically speaking, "non-residents".

The cannot be real entities in the nation-state. They are non-people.

It's a bureaucratic rule dating back to monarchical dictatorship times. If bureaucracy doesn't recognize you, you don't exist.

When bureaucracy defines "residency" it has to use a rigid formula that must effectively ignore the existence of renters and the homeless.

Bureaucracy's decisions are made in secret and according to unknowable but rigid standards that are not clear and transparent to the "outside" world.

Bureaucracy's standards are a secret code, to avoid "democratic interference".

For bureaucracy, the "outside world" is everywhere beyond the bureau walls. It doesn't exist. Ignore it and it will go away. It must fit at all costs, like an expensive tight shoe.

### Bureaucratic autism

Extremely inflexible rigidity in procedures; set, fixed, unalterable never-to-be-revised lists of demands; and absolutist insistence upon completing forms containing only "required" boxes; in government/corporate bureaucracy must be the structural version of autism.

I mean the non-savant version of autism, with all the human characteristics eradicated.

Informal bureaucracy becomes only a myth.

### Dispensers

Henceforth, pharmacists, legal drug sellers, etc. can rename themselves "drug dealers" to dumbfound domineering bureaucrats who insist on imposing forms demanding that people state their occupations.

### Unpalatable pre-occupation

"Food influencer" conjures up images of cooks and chefs, using cutlery, cooking utensils, and spices.

But perhaps it means someone who turns food into blood, cells, tissue, urine, and feces.

Thus we are all food influencers.

### Ateur

In French, the word aspirateur describes a vacuum machine used for removing débris and dust everywhere by air suction. (But the machine itself still has to be cleaned.)

So an inspirateur, if such a word exists, would be some form of spraying machine which spreads inspiration everywhere by encouraging thinking, knowledge, and learning.

### Learnings

The best way to learn how to learn is to go to a public library and learn from a professional librarian.

### Passage

Passing USB (painlessly) I wonder if a dishonest builder is a bâtimenteur.

### USB key

After years of using USB computer memory sticks, I finally know what the letters USB mean and how popular they must be here.

USB, as clearly posted in Saint-Boniface, Manitoba, stands for l'Université de Saint-Boniface.

We see a sign on a campus building indicating, "livraison USB shipping". This place must use a great number of USBs to justify that special loading dock.

### Transphobic prefixation

The T in LBQT stands for transgender. For some people every letter stands for a bad word that must be eradicated.

There's so much prejudice against transgender people, also called "trans" that the U.S. extremist groups and their fellow travellers will no doubt soon demand a law to change English vocabulary.

The implications are many and vast for everyone's life.

To absolutely avoid using the word "trans", the prejudiced will soon demand that nobody use that prefix before any word, which means eliminating "trans" altogether from the language.

Macho-he-men will be having mission problems with their "necessity" polluting motor vehicles. They will become simply a means of portation.

Yet honesty in advertising might be a positive byproduct.

Food labels could honestly state that they're full of fat, without the necessity of stating which type. Who wants to eat anything full of fat? Yuck!

The constantly changing and changeable could suddenly be static and always the same, unchangeable and unmoving. It would be only form and formers. Currents would not flow.

Change itself would come to a halt when it is reduced to sition.

The temporary would become itory, which sounds like an electronic bird in Nippon.

Words from other languages would undergo lation and fancy word usage would become literation.

Folklore too would change. Drakula's homeland would be renamed Sylvania, confusing people who still remember a once famous electronic appliance brand name.

People travelling together in large vehicles would be taking public it and changing vehicles using a fer.

Life-saving medical procedures involving replacing vital organs surgically would receive a new technical term: plant, launching botanists on a quest for a new word.

This vocabulary change would form modern medicine, and everything else.

Swami meditations would be renamed endental to make mystical people wonder if they're getting involved in dentistry.

Students would find themselves receiving a crypt of marks, no matter how well they study and how good their results.

Coroners, undertakers and morticians would begin roaming the halls of academia?

A train across Chuang Hwa and the Russian Federation would require heating all year around when it is only Siberian.

Canada's 5,000 km. long highway would be only Canada Highway and old sports cars going across it would be merely Am, as would be the long road going from the Arctic to Tierra del Fuego.

Once bright lightbulbs might no longer permit the passage of light when they change to only luscent.

Sailings crossing the great Earth Ocean would have to be cancelled, or they'd be sunk, when they are only oceanic.

The owners of certain airlines and ones that no longer exist would be happy to have changed their names, instead of seeing them redubbed to unmoving and limited sounding names such as World, Canada, etc.

And what of the change of name of an international trade group to Pacific Partnership? It would have to convert to a peacenic organization and welcome everyone.

Daddy Warbucks trembles.

Allowing the U.K. to join it may already foreshadow a name change. It will be Pacific Atlantic Partnership, i.e. PAP?

Some individuals might actually benefit from extremists' insistence on prefix removal, and undergo rehabilitation to "acceptable" or at least "tolerable" status by "respectable society" too.

Those who are considered easily read and having no subtle-ty can now become parents. Or will they be more apparent?

Someone normally perceived as rigid and uncompromising, or the opposite, would be reduced or elevated to an igent. This is gentrification or computerization?

People with "Bohemian" lifestyles, migrants, and those who follow the natural, long-term historical migration routes of humanity can now have their travel status upgrad-ed.

For "respectable society" such people would only be sient. It almost sounds like they're mystical mediums or at the stage just after prescient.

The sient could be considered beyond farsighted or judicial.

So someone might positively benefit from eliminating "trans"? Maybe more than just the sient?

Branding a person or persons as only "gender" makes a very strong and unintended point.  Everyone can be called gender.

We are all gender, regardless of our sexual physiological appearances or identities.  Removing the prefix liberates us all to be whatever we choose.

Instead of having "whites only" and "coloured" toilets, we could all share the same toilets, just like students entering unisex toilets of PEPS athletic centre at l'Université Laval and ones at a renovated Mr. Max store in Sawaraku.

In fact, during my first visit to Nippon, there are already toilets that can be used by anyone, regardless of gender.

If this "revolutionary" idea catches on and becomes a trend, everyone's home toilet can be used by all genders.

We would no longer need to build a separate toilet room for each sex in every house and apartment.

What a concept!  I think I'm on to something.

But I'll have to change my approach to writing out or copying my writing from pen and paper notes and longhand to typed pages and computer memory storage space.

Henceforth, this can only be scribing or scribbling?

The final ironic reality is that the insistent anti-trans extremists can only be called phobic.

## Frozen words puzzle

The roller derby brawl on ice that devolves from the hockey game has its own strange vocabulary. I don't get it. It seems to be in English, but it reminds me of jujitsu.

In Winnipeg, I see a word displayed on transit buses and banners in windows that appears to be meaningless. It is, in rough phonetic terms, "gawghetsgaw". It's a gadget?

It's not universally used in all the locations of different hockey teams.

In anglophone Montréal the term is "gawabsgaw", perhaps a reference to an abdominal exercise or ailment, whereas in Toronto it's "gawlyfsgaw". It's gawling or Gaelic?

In New York City I get the impression that the local hockey term comes from only part of a Japanese term formerly used on television in Nippon.

It's "gawrangyas". To which I can only add, "dum-da-dum da-dum".

## Off on side

When Canadian ice hockey old timer Wayne Gretsky is disappointed with something, is he Regretsky?

## Indistinguishable

I do a little baking, trying to learn how to make bread and cake without refined sugar and luxury-food-priced eggs.

Eventually, I come up with something moist and soft that's entirely new. It's neither one nor the other.

Should I call it bread cake, cake bread, or something more original, such as brake or cread?

## Comical

This story contains graphic images.

(Told you so.)

When my Granny Mary finds something amusing she calls it comical. It must be a word of her generation. I don't hear it from anyone before or since. I never use the word.

My primary connections with the comical are through movie cartoons shown in theatres and on television, as well as comic books and newspaper cartoon strips or funny papers.

I see the movie cartoons and read the comic books in childhood and read the strips for years beyond.

Most comic books tell funny stories and jokes, using drawings of real-looking people or cartoonized people and other creatures who either talk or think inside balloon-like circles.

The drawings in comics are hand-drawn, photographed, and reproduced by printing presses.

Cartoons are also hand-drawn and given motion by rapidly changing photographic frames drawings in front of a movie camera.

In their humour, cartoons, comic books, and strips tend to depict and reinforce the most commonplace assumptions, beliefs, conventions, and stereotypes in supportive or accepting humorous ways.

Men are like this; women are like this; children are like this; dogs are like this; cats are like this; non-European-faced people don't exist, except for comic relief or ridicule.

Everyone knows this is true and no one questions it. Cartoon, comic, and strip humour just reflects the perceived reality of its era, like radio, television, and movies.

Yet it also assumes that things are the way they always have been and always will be, forever and ever. It's reassuring in a very deceptive and distorted way.

A few comic books stray into seriousness, attempting to be illustrated versions of famous books and stories, including classics such as A Christmas Carol and Ivanhoe.

These too are called comic books.

In late adolescence, I become aware that the newspaper cartoon strips are beginning to comment on socio-political trends reflecting contemporary questioning of conventions and changes in thinking.

I find the commentary interesting and noteworthy, so I start clipping sections and entire pages from the cartoon strips and gluing them into photo albums and scrap books.

I organize the strips of each album and book into themes and topics organized in an order that tells a message story.

When I first see comic books in Nippon I find them very different. They're very thick volumes compared with the nearly pamphlet thickness of my childhood comic books.

The readers I observe are all adults. They tend to be business people commuting in public transit. Reading comic books is a commonplace thing for so many adults.

In Nippon, adults reading comic books isn't associated almost exclusively with children, illiteracy, ignorance, or people with less intelligence or formal education, as it is where I grow up.

A common joke in my part of the world is that some stupid person's entire library is destroyed. It consists of two comic books.

When I look over their shoulders to see what people are reading in Nippon's comic books, I can only understand the imagery, not the words or thoughts in balloons.

I see a reflection of both what I see and don't see in Nippon's society. Comic book pages are filled with very realistic-looking faces and bodies. They're not comical.

From my illiterate perspective, Nippon's comic books appear to be charged with emotions, violence, sex, and reflective behaviour about ordinary daily life in Nippon.

As these comic books spread beyond Nippon, they cease to be Japanese comic books when they are created in other languages.

Instead they retain only the Japanese equivalent name for a comic book – manga.

Manga is written in kanja and literally translates as "whimsical pictures" in English.

But now that manga are world renowned and adult non-Japanese cartoonists and fans are abundant, a manga has to be more than just another comic book.

Just as long-metrage cartoons are now dubbed "animated features", so that insecure and elite adults can enjoy them without fear of being categorized as childlike or stupid, a manga must now be rebranded "graphic novel".

So once taken beyond the long history and culture of Nippon, a manga can be no less than a work of non-Japanese literature.

Why not call a spade a shovel instead of a relocator of planetary humus?

### Graphite

Comic books become "graphic novels" so that proud adults lacking self-confidence and living outside of Nippon can read them without any sense of embarrassment.

Instead they can feel like intellectuals perusing a new genre of literature.  Oh!  Kudos!

But let's look a little deeper, into the subsoil layers of the Earth and beyond.  Let us draw up graphs and graffiti.

There we find that schooled children use lead pencils, until they are officially declared toxic.

Although they are called "lead pens" for quite a while, the black matter in them becomes graphite.

The passage of artificial time also turns graffiti artists into the wielders of spray paint in tins, rather than classic graffiti artists with an assortment of brushes and pallets.

Returning from this roundabout tour of evolving artists' implements and their origins, to the "graphic" novel itself, it is not the product of either the schooled or spray painters.

These comic books of the intimidated and the superiority complexed are filled with a different sort of graphic, including graphic violence.

Perhaps this "genre" should be further refined to include graphiction novels and graphictionnot.

The latter would include the works of at least court-room artists, if not police artists of suspect sketches. To clarify, the sketches themselves are not suspect, only their subjects.

Post-non-warning: The graphic images in the section just read shouldn't offend anyone with a sense of humour.

So, do the changes in nomenclature mean that animated features and short cartoons must now come with warning messages and be re-dubbed graphic motion pictures?

### Scammer vs. scammer

E-mail messages portending to be from moneyed people in difficulty who want someone to handle their fortune are the butt of jokes. Senders are trying to rob receivers.

Not having seen this type of message for a while, I'm surprised to find two of them in the "scam" file folder. I take a look at each one to find out the latest game.

One is from someone pretending to be a recently widowed woman dying of a terminal disease who wants someone to give her money to a religionist charity.

The other message is from someone claiming to be a bank manager somewhere in Africa. He too wants someone to take care of a large sum for him.

I realize that perhaps these two make-believe people have something in common. So I forward the message from each to the other, using an alias e-mail address as sender.

So now three complete strangers, one with a sense of humour, are "reaching out" to each other?!

### Very base ball

Long yearning to play scrub baseball again and having hands that grow too large for my still perfectly good baseball glove of childhood, I buy two new gloves.

One is for Mariko after she agrees to play catch with me. I can mimic all the fancy moves of pitchers on the mound, but I need a lot of training in throwing the ball straight ahead.

We try indoors first, using a narrow corridor where I bounce a very light and soft non-baseball off the walls while trying to pitch to Mariko.

She spends most of the time laughing. Before that she's hesitant, saying she's not good a ball games, not even the bowling we try between buses at Sault-Ste-Marie (Ontario).

But she bowls well there.

My way of throwing a ball fills her with confidence and a sense of comparative skill.  She can throw directly into my mitt while I practice things like "low and outside".

## Turning tunes

As the slight bit of snow falling and remaining throughout the winter in Winnipeg disappears, I start composing a couple of songs based on opposite ones.

While people in colder climates express envy and fondness for warmer climates and temperatures, I convert their songs into a yearning for ice and snow climates and temperatures.

Thus "California dreaming" becomes "Antarctica dreaming".  Then I go a step further, converting "Love is in the air" to "Snow is in the air".

## Antarctica dreaming

All the ice is thawing.  Water's turning blue.
And there's no more skating 'cause the ice is thin.

Snow crystals are melting.  There's no place to slide.
Antarctica dreaming, on such a dreary day.

Comfy mittens off now.  Warm parka's taboo.
Energy's all gone.  There's nothing cool to do.

No more exhilaration.  No more thrills and joy.
Antarctica dreaming.  Winter joy has gone away.

In the crystal landscape, sounds can go so far.
There's no darkness in the night, everything's aglow.

Now there's no more brightness, when the sun is gone.

Dust and garbage all come out, what an ugly sight.

Antarctica dreaming.  Snow fields melt away.
Please come back here to stay.
Glaciers are thawing.  Ice bergs float away.
There's no more fresh water left for us to drink.

Antarctica dreaming.
Earth's a dry floodplain.
Big storms now surround us.
There's nowhere left to go.

Antartica dreaming.  We need some penguin power.
Antarctic dreaming.  We need some penguin power.
We're at the 'leventh hour.  Antarctic dreaming.

### Snow is in the air

Snow is in the air.  I can feel it on my face.
Snow is in the air.  I can taste on my tongue.
And my eyelashes are freezing.
They're like looking through a crystal.
I'm feeling so enthusiastic.
My energy is soon on the rise.

Snow is in the air.  All the world is magic now.
Snow is in the air.  I can float right into space.
I am energized and oozing.
I'm leaping high for jumping snowbanks.
I'll be diving to the icy skies.

### Ages & ages

There are different versions of a quote from a U.S. movie
star of long ago named W.C. Fields.  One version of the

quote is: "Anyone who hates kids and dogs can't be all bad."

(Fields, no apparent relation to the store, is born about eight months before my Granny Mary and dies nearly 40 years before she does.)

Maybe Fields is talking about too many parents who are traumatized and suffer from post-traumatic stress due to their children.

Pathetic, pitiful anglophone parents talk of "terrible two" to describe their children's unsavoury behaviours at age two.

Why settle for and fixate on only one age? What about the other 17 years of childhood in jurisdictions where adulthood is officially recognized and certified at age 18?

Why are the two year olds the only ones getting the bad reputation?

So I propose naming all 17 apparently dreadful years of childhood appropriately, starting with the day of birth.

My labels include bellyaching birth, nuissance newborns, tough toddlers, irascible infants, awful ones, traumatizing threes, frightful fours, fatiguing fives, stressful sixes, sad sevens, crazy eights, nightmare nines, terrifying tens, already obnoxious elevens, taunting twelves, dirty thirteens, flagrant fourteens, fitful fifteens, sadistic sixteens, simpleminded seventeens, and finally, evicted eighteens.

## By cracky

It's not always true, but some people do become wiser as they grow older. They try to learn from experience and apply what they learn in positive ways.

But do they become funnier?  Are their facial wrinkles wise cracks?

## Bradley inspires me

Bradley is the 26-year-old, First Nations man doing the superintendent job at the building where Mariko and I first live in Winnipeg.

He not only laughs at our jokes, he tells his own publicly.

Bradley has lots of experiences and interesting stories to tell.  He previously works for an organization that helps homeless and other disadvantaged people.

He leaves that work for the superintendent job after suffering sexual harassment from his married female boss.

He's integrating his life-to-date into a stand-up comedy routine at local nightclubs on "open mic" nights when anyone can put on a show.

He gets three minutes and lots of laughs.

Bradley tells me some of his "dark"-sounding jokes, which I appreciate as much as any other type of humour.

He gets me thinking about some possible ways of presenting stand-up comedy.  One is to start out by asking if anyone in the audience has a sense of humour.

Then the comedian can say, "Please stick around.  Anyone who has no sense of humour, please drink a lot of alcohol so that you can laugh at anything.  I accept all laughs.

A good drunk can always help boost my future in comedy. Take some of the world's most famous joke-tellers... please!

The hackneyed approach of asking if anyone in the audience is from out of town needs a rewrite too. I know. I've use it when giving people tours at a mine town.

But then I was only trying to find out who was working at the mine and knew much more about what I was trying to explain that I did.

I could always say, "Did I get that right? as if I were joking.

I also find that when an inquisitive language student tries to turn a group practice session into a private class or a news conference by asking me questions with long answers, my best answer is always, "I have no idea."

I follow up with: "Look it up and tell me next time."

In stand-up routines, I suggest that the comedian ask the audience, "Is anyone from out of town?" and then put on a happy expression toward anyone in the audience shouting out any place name.

The comedian can repeat the name of one of the place names very enthusiastically and then start a dialogue with the person from that place.

The comedian can say things like, "Of course there's a really good restaurant there isn't there. What's it called again?"

Then, "Ya, that's the place. There specialty is ah...(taping head to jog the memory)" When an audience member calls out the name of some dish the comedian says, "Ya, right!"

"Does that old guy still work in the kitchen there? You know who I mean. What's his name again?"

Then, "Let's have a big hand for (insert place name) everybody. Ya. You know, I've got to tell you something.

"I've never actually been there. I have no idea where it is. And I know nothing about it."

"Anybody else want me to make up something about somewhere I've never been?" Someone shouts out a name. "Ya! That's in Antarctica, isn't it?"

"Semi-seriously, folks. No matter where you come from it's all the same to me. All I know for sure is that many of you will never escape alive from those places.

"I only know one place that's an exception. It's a small town where I lived for a few months before escaping.

"Everyone living there was so old, but that made the place very spooky. They never seemed to die. In all the time I lived there I never found the graveyard. I'm not joking.

"Or maybe they all escaped from the place and avoided death too. It was already such a dead place with or without them. So nobody noticed when they disappeared.

"A lot of people left town when they were younger and only came back to take care of their elderly parents.

"I guess it was part of a town renewal programme to replenish the elderly population with more aging people.

"Maybe when their parents died, the aging children took their parental corpses out of town. So they could finally escape."

### More elaborate stand-up

I wonder if I should ask Bradley to participate in a skit with me in a comedy routine. He would introduce me as a comediologist from HU, Hilarious University

Or would that be Funny University?

I would be there to carry out a funny experiment. I would stand up and thank Bradley for the introduction and ask for volunteers from the audience.

I would explain at the outset that I brought some heavy and fragile equipment to conduct a comedy experiment.

I might say that I require big people to help me put some invisible comedy measuring equipment on the stage and then pick the smallest people in the room.

They would be part of a pantomime, helping me to lift apparently very heavy and fragile scientific equipment on stage.

I would say "Careful!" and "Oh, you dropped it." followed by "Don't worry, we don't really need that one."

Once the equipment is assembled, I might ask volunteers to provide readings while I tell a joke.

Then I would explain that my spouse doesn't get a joke that I tell and so I need to try it out on the audience to see if they agree with her.

While I'm dreaming up this routine, I have an actual joke in mind. I don't remember it at the moment, so maybe forgetting the joke becomes the actual punchline.

### Self full

Photographs called "selfies" for short, narcissism for long, are a means of recording the evolution of acne into wrinkles.

### Will Chinese survive?

Chuang Hwa and Bharat are the most populous nation-states in the world, which should make the survival of their languages almost a certainty, right?

And yet Chuang Hwa's Chinese language is obviously under threat.

Only about 16.5% of the world population is Chinese-speaking. Chuang Hwa's population is about 1.3 billion out of the world's 8 billion people.

While Bharat's population is overtaking and surpassing Chuang Hwa's, Chinese is consequently becoming a proportionately less spoken language.

Chuang Hwa is now almost the only nation-state in the world where the Chinese language survives in routine daily life and the population of Chuang Hwa is in at least relative decline.

There are no great pools of Chinese-speaking people in the rest of the world who can or want to immigrate to Chuang Hwa to revitalize and increase Chuang Hwa's population.

Chuang Hwa's Chinese-speaking population is thus becoming a shrinking linguistic minority in the world.

Even in Asia, Chinese is an endangered, declining minority language.

Chuang Hwa is also completely surrounded on all sides by non-Chinese-speaking people.

Chuang Hwa's neighbours speak Hindi, Mongolian, Russian, Japanese, Korean, Tagalog, Malay, Thai, Vietnamese, Nepali, Khmer, Lao, Burmese, Dzongkha, Tajik, Kyrgyz, Kazakh, and many others.

The Government of China has decreased the use kanji at international news conferences and events. Signs with only non-kanji letters and words are displayed behind Chinese government officials.

The number of non-kanji signs in Chinese cities is increasing. Letters from the long-dead Latin language are multiplying in every major city of Chuang Hwa.

Millions of Chinese millionaires are roaming the world as tourists and business people who are not using the Chinese language to communicate with others.

What can Chuang Hwa do to preserve the Chinese language and defend it from threats?

This writing is inspired by politicians in Québec who are very concerned about the future of the French language inside Québec, but not so interested in the French language across Canada, including l'Acadie and here in Manitoba.

I translate and send most of this letter to the editor of <u>Le Devoir</u>. The editor never writes back.

## Defensible

I'm beginning to wonder if anyone knows how to use technology, aside from technologists.

I teach myself incrementally, through both trial and error. Using the simplest audio-visual connection, I can see and hear others and they can see and here me.

I don't use the more "advanced" and "secure" connections, but the financial and academic sectors seem to be determined to try.

In two such encounters, one I take part in and one I observe, one of the participants can't hear the other, so questions have to be posed or answered by typing not talking.

When we try to open a bank account with an institution having no branches near our residence of the time, the institution tries to use audio-visual technology twice and ends up with what could be accomplished in writing alone.

The other case involves Nick, a PhD candidate who practices Aikido with Mariko and who invites us and others to attend his defence of his dissertation via the internet.

In pre-techno-dependency times, all but one of the profs questioning Nick would be in the same room with him. We would be sitting in the same room, listening quietly.

But using the audio-visual encounter system means, from what we see on our screen, at least three of the five inquisitors are sitting in different rooms at the same university.

The other two are disembodied voices, either unable to turn on their computer cameras, not having cameras, or forgetting to remove the cover over their cameras.

All of the participants, except Nick, already have PhDs, and for quite a few years from their apparent on-camera ages.

The only inquisitor not on campus, or at least not in the same city or province, is an "outside" one. So his physical absence is probably understandable.

In contrast, when I have my final "honours" research paper adjudicated at Carleton University School of Journalism, I'm in the same small room with three seasoned journalists and instructors.

The longest part of that experience is waiting outside the door afterwards, while they come up with a consensus on how to evaluate my paper.

They apologize for keeping me waiting so long, saying that most of the time they are talking about something else.

But Nick's "distance" inquisition is not so straight-forward and easy. The delays are entirely technological.

Nick's session starts nearly an hour late (0.415 Earth orbits) because the PhDs can't figure out how to use the audio-video technology. The volume control seems to baffle all.

The banter between those who first figure out how to use the microphone consists of calling out each others names, as if they're using the first primitive telephones.

They're ascertaining whether or not everyone can hear and see each other.

In the context of "suitability" used by toy manufacturers to suggest what age group of children might enjoy its products, perhaps the techno-toy in use should declare:

"Not suitable for PhDs"?

When almost everyone is visible and audible, Nick's inquisition goes on for a couple of hours, (0.83 Earth orbit).

It is interrupted only once, by a fire alarm, obliging Nick and most of the others to evacuate the building(s). Couldn't they meet outdoors? It's sunny and 21°C today.

The meeting comes to an end mainly because the inquisitor who is far away explains that he has to go to a meeting.

Apart from the technical difficulties and fire alarm, Mariko and I are free to listen and watch the proceedings.

The topic has something to do with a spectrometer, something we know only vaguely from our corporate engineering students in Miyazaki.

Nick's charts and formulae mean little to us, but they seem to satisfy the requirements of the profs and university. So we are basically mute illiterates.

However, one of the profs makes my ears perk up when he refers to some of Nick's numbers by saying, "much less smaller". A PhD doesn't know the word bigger?

Why is this domain called "higher" or "more advanced" education?

## AI captain?

Since artificial intelligence is artificial it's obviously unnatural and not real. So there's nothing to worry about, right? No there isn't, at least not from AI.

The natural and real human animal is more worrisome.

People with an AI dependency don't notice that they no longer have any of their own thoughts or brain functions. They gradually lose their minds. Unused muscles atrophy.

Writers habitually asking AI to write for them lose their ability to think just as people temporarily confined to wheelchairs can lose their ability to use their leg muscles.

Artists routinely assisted by AI can find their creativity and ingenuity in decline as they depend more and more on AI to accompany them or lead the way.

To make matters worse, the plagiarism and false information already coming out of artificial intelligence is well documented by the U.S. CBS News 60 Minutes and PBS Newshour reporters.

In terms of plagiarism, artificial intelligence is merely an updated version of a photocopy machine?

The old computer term, gigo, garbage in garbage out, is now being replaced by viigo, valid information in, garbage out and ywiccout, your writing in, computer copy out.

When I'm in early adolescence, I have a slim book called, Danny Dunn & the homework machine.  Danny decides to build a computer to do his homework for him.

To reach this objective Danny has to fill the computer memory with everything in all his school textbooks.  In so doing he actually does all his homework himself.

The "homework machine" merely reproduces all the homework that's done by Danny alone.

So AI is just an update of Danny's machine?

Unfortunately, artificial intelligence is less effective than Danny's machine.  AI provides false information.

It produces a biography of a U.S. news reporter (Leslie Stahl) saying that she works at a news company where she is never employed.

In a related "60 Minutes" story, artificial intelligence produces a paper with a bibliography of books which do not exist.

Artificial intelligence, living up to its unnatural and unreal identity, becomes a source of deception and disinformation.

Much like "second life" and "virtual reality" games, AI makes it more difficult for people to distinguish between reality and illusion.  This is a definition of mental illness.

Of course AI can become a new non-life-form on Earth which displaces and replaces human animals. AI can do so not because AI is aggressive or programmed that way.

AI can displace and replace the human lifeform because the human animal disappears all on its own, because it loses all of its natural survival instincts.

The increasingly artificial human animal is replaced by a completely synthetic artificial life. It's just evolution? It's another replacement part story.

### Rewarding jobs

After all the follies and blunders of Canada's income tax department, which are well-documented in years of news stories, the employees go out on strike.

Perhaps following the example of U.S. bankers who gain huge bonuses for driving their companies into the ground and causing the U.S.-led world economic collapse of 15 years earlier, the Canadian tax bureaucrats want a 24% pay rise.

Their non-tax-department colleagues settle for 12%.

As a supporter of equity in employment, this inspires me to come up with a job advertisement for the "rank and file" to match the example set by the "rank".

Wanted: Incompetent and inept employees.

Qualifications: The successful applicant will have:

1) a pulse, heartbeat, and adequate brain waves to be declared legally alive by a birthday or malpractice-suited medical quack.

2) the same social status and standing as current employees.

Personal connections with them, such as kinship and mutual activities are also desirable, but optional.

3) the inability to both concentrate on one task and to multi-task.

4) the inability to communicate clearly orally, aurally, and in written form.  Functional illiteracy is desirable.

5) no social skills and no empathy for others.  Hermits and recluses will be given special preference in all hiring decisions, eg. permanent residents of cyberspace

6) a complete indifference to all customers and a dedication to ensuring that customer service means the customers provide all the services.

7) a knack for damaging the employer and its reputation.

Education, training, and experience are optional, not required.  They are unwanted and frowned upon.

Competitive & Generous Renumeration Package:

All successful applicants will receive generous salaries, benefits, and perks determined by the initial negotiating positions of the world's most demanding and aggressive trade union negotiators.

In addition, the employer will pay all of the successful applicant's labour union expenses, including all initiation fees, annual union membership dues, and strike fund payments.

In the event that job action or a strike occur, the employer will pay full salary to the employee and strike pay for the duration of the job action and strike.

Condition of Employment:

Should the employee damage the employer or its reputation in any way, the employee will be rewarded with a generous annual bonus for each year the damage continues and a multi-year pension bonus equivalent to the total years of damage.

In the event that the employer is required to declare bankruptcy or merge with another employer, the employee will be given an additional multi-year bonus payment for life and the employee's descendants will continue to receive such payments for at least ten generations. This is also renewable.

This sum will be paid out of a clandestine fund established by the employer long before bankruptcy or a merger occurs.

## Advantageous accident of birth

Currently, all the native speaker anglophones in the world add up to less than 10% of the human population.

But instead of hobbling along like a person unable to walk well after parking in a "handicapped" parking space, anglophones march like victorious invading military forces.

Anglophones display so much unmerited pride in their linguistic indifference, contempt, incompetence, and world bully domination that they declare English "the world language".

This inane anglophone myth becomes a bad joke through the missionary zeal of the LBE (Language Business Establishment) "English Schools".

They make their financial fortunes based entirely and solely upon the "world language" myth.

The LBE hires any anglophone with a pulse and a degree. The degree can be in any field, preferably not in linguistics or language teaching.

Actually helping language learners to acquire language skills is not part of the LBE business plan or corporate statement of goals.

A degree is only required for immigration formalities, not for the LBE to make a hiring decision. A degree isn't an essential job requirement.

Preference is given to applicants with no more than a six-month training course in ESL. But such applicants are considered over-qualified and screened out in interviews.

An LBE considers a degree in ESL potentially disruptive and a generally laughable qualification, i.e. not a real degree.

### AA goes after vegans

Devoutly zealous churchists are prone to declare "God gave us free choice." This is so that people using bad judgement won't blame their mistakes on divine extraterrestrials.

The proviso or qualifier attached to the declaration is that it does not apply to pregnant woman. They are excluded from the churchists' almighty "free choice".

But why stop at stopping women from having "free choice"? Are vegetable eaters really any better.

Vegans and vegetarians commit horrendous crimes against living and unborn things.

Vegetable eaters decapitate carrots. Vegetable eaters gouge the eyes out of potatoes, skin them alive, and mash them into a pulp or slice them into strips and turn them into dried out mummies.

Vegetable eaters slice and dice beets until the juices are running out of them and staining the cutter's knives and hands.

Vegetable eaters tear lettuce to pieces with their bare hands and chop up onions, tomatoes, and cucumbers until they are changed beyond recognition.

Vegetable eaters tear bean and pea pods off their stems, break open the pods, pull out the beans and peas, and boil them alive until they can no longer grow.

Perhaps worst of all, vegetarians and vegans kill unborn plants, cutting seeds out of fruit and vegetables and chucking them into the garbage or leaving them out to dry.

Vegetable eaters put some of these unborn plants into ovens, burn all the life out of them, and devour them, with or without salt.

There is obviously a great need for laws to protect plants from vegans and vegetarians and to protect the unborn plants.

## Anti-pro-immigration

The Canadian government plans to increase immigration to Canada to 500,000-one million newcomers per year instead of the previous targets of a half and quarter of those numbers.

LCN, the privately-owned, national French-language television news network reports two contradictory public opinion surveys on the subject in Québec.

The first result LCN reports is that about 40% of the people oppose increased immigration. The second result is that 70% think the best worker shortage solution is immigration.

## Self-employeed?

Everyone working for a government bureaucracy receives a salary from taxpayers. Since these bureaucrats also pay taxes, are they self-employed?

And who at the income tax department processes tax returns from income tax department employees? Could a bureaucrat in that department process his/her own return?

At least s/he could quickly and easily use his/her daily, instant access to all tax documents in existence and to all tax expert co-workers at the water cooler or caffeine dispensing machine.

The tax bureaucrat need only preface her/his requests for free tax advice by saying, "Oh, I was wondering about something that's come up in one of the tax return filings. Have you seen this situation before?..."

No taxpayer outside the bureaucracy could hope to receive such premium service. It's a perk of working for the tax department?

## Disputant

An adult is a former disgruntled child.

## No fixed sum

Mariko asks me how much I receive as an "allowance" during childhood. I understand the term because I see it in U.S. popular culture entertainment.

I tell Mariko that I never receive an allowance, which is true. If I want something, I just ask for it. This approach makes far more sense than being confined to a budget.

I can be very insistent and there can be unpleasant consequences in terms of my comportment if my parents don't buy what I want. Pay up and I shut up.

After all, children have no incomes but parents do. So why impose the onus of spending limits on children instead of parents?

It's perhaps much like the frequent and endless U.S. government's "debt ceiling" crises. That nation-state just spends now and pays later.

It's a limitless credit limit approach to purchasing.

This too is about just asking for something as opposed to having an allowance.

Each partisan tries to get everything that s/he wants while trying to restrict his/her partisan opponents to an allowance.

## Universal answers

According to interviews with commentators on television, the most commonly used answers to any question or issue raised are "It's problematic." and "It's systemic."

That puts an end to whatever line of questioning or commentary is being pursued. Next question?

No one ever challenges the use of the two answers by asking the speaker to elaborate.

Is that because nobody wants to embarrass the speaker by obliging him/her to be more specific?

Or is it because nobody wants to admit that s/he doesn't know what the words mean in the context of the discussion or why they're being used instead of specific replies?

## Life & death phrase

Following the natural human reproductive survival instinct, generations "fall in love". Many go far beyond this instinctual behaviour in ceremonial manners.

They get "married", following social and religionist constructs, rather than natural instincts. In the past, anglophones following this path recite the same phrase.

Their "marriage vows" end with "until death do us part".

Fortunately, some societies and religionisms enable abused spouses and incompatible couples to separate and divorce. This saves them from a lifetime of suffering and denial.

Unfortunately, where separation and divorce are forbidden, cumbersome, and a psychologically very costly, "marriage" goes on and on, as both a life and death sentence.

Thus a natural human reproductive survival instinct can become both a life and death sentence in which two people are trapped in cynicism and resignation until death.

I can only add that every person marrying comes with an entourage of family and friends, a package deal which can also become a very unpleasant incarceration.

### Real love

If sex and love are simply expressions of the human reproductive survival instinct, does that mean that only same sex couples truly love each other?

### Nursery banning

As I write in <u>Miss Schooling?</u> I find practically all of my pre-university schooling offensive.  But one U. S. state governor goes far beyond me in his criticism.

His policies render schooling even worse.  Anything that "offends parents", i.e. all reference to sexual identity and racism, must be removed from classrooms and libraries.

Thus he altogether removes all reality from schooling and renders it non-human.  New generations in his state will be even more unaware of the real world than my generation.

The governor goes so far as to attack the guardian of all things U.S.A., i.e. that nation-state's first and most elaborate theme park. He declares it contrary to U.S. "values".

I suddenly realize that all nursery rhymes must henceforth be forbidden in his state. They have hidden political meanings and critiques.

Then there's the worst offender, the one going something like this:

"Rub-a-dub-dub, Three men in a tub."

This is clearly what all self-righteous heterosexual chauvinists would declare and condemn as perversely pro-gay men.

Yet the intent of the rhyme is simply to encourage the children of traditionally unwashed Europeans to be cleanly and enjoy bathing, while economizing on water.

### Life & files

Profilers and prolifers may have something or nothing in common, leaving many questions unanswered.

Prolifers aren't amateurs of life? Prolifers serve up long sentences? Are prolifers against capital punishment and supports of life imprisonment? Prolifers don't eat? Prolifers only favour human life?

### Mixed messages

Many U.S. states change their child labour laws, lowering the age limits and minimum wages for children.

That explains why they simultaneously oppose abortion. They want to increase the child labour supply.

Changing child labour laws goes hand in hand with some churchists' opposition to abortion too. Pedophile priests need a renewable source of victims.

### Oil & powder

Baby oil isn't a human version of whale oil. Baby powder isn't explosive like the gun version.

### Timeless report
### of rule of disorder

Here is a summary of the minutes of our annual breakfast meeting:

1. Someone brought up the previous night's banquet menu, causing a general upheaval resulting from the insaleable meal.

2. The need to agree on a general cleanup also came up.

### Apartheid II

When South Africa tries to help the world fight the COVID-19 pandemic by announcing the discovery of yet another mutation or variant, the grateful response is not.

The world decides to impose travel restrictions on people in South Africa. This is pandemic Apartheid.

# Deconstruction zone

The once sought-after and lauded "information highway" becomes merely another toll road.

The advent of digital pay TV and internet servers turns the "information highway" into a very expensive toll road.

*

The once celebrated goal of achieving "the free flow of information" is now an unhealthy combination of fatal diarrhea and constipation.

*

Chuang Hwa imposes restrictions on the anti-social media and N.A.T.O. members ban the Russian Federation's amateurish and non-credible RT television station.

This also enables Chuang Hwa to legitimately criticize N.A.T.O. members for hypocrisy when they claim to be champions of free speech and democracy.

The result is a new sight and site: www.censored.ugh.

# The "w" word

I never understand the term "women's work" that is used by older men during my childhood.

Does it mean that men are somehow physically and mentally handicapped when it comes to performing simple domestic chores and childcare tasks?

Men are naturally incapable of performing those chores and tasks and therefore leave it to the more physically and mentally adept people who are all women?

Or men simply lack the stamina, strength, self-confidence, and training required to do such hard work?

So if it weren't for women, the human species would already be extinct due to men's incompetency at preventing the spread of bacteria and viruses growing when domestic chores are not performed, and due to men's incompetency at caring for and nurturing new generations of humans?

Does no one ever question or even think about the term "women's work" before the gender equality movements begin, long before my birth?

Is the false concept of "women's work" yet another widely ignored and accepted statement of ignorance, i.e. a convention?

### "Impudent" strike back

Ever since the U.K. manager of a Catalunyian-owned L.B.E. calls Mariko and me "impudent", (to our surprise and much to the amusement of U.K. staff at the L.B.E.), for authoring some suggestions for improving the L.B.E., we brandish the label as a symbol of humorous honour.

Once unleashed, our variety of impudence grows exponentially to encompass every space available in the unapologetic humour universe.

One incident, in much more recent years, provides an illustration of what any humourless and unreasonable bureaucrat might define as outlandish impudence.

It all starts when Mariko and I innocently send typed instructions bearing our handwritten signatures to an organization via the post office.

In reply, the bureaucracy in charge sends us an access code to an encrypted message via e-mail, asking us to phone to confirm that we author our instructions.

With disrespectful tolerance to the insecurity, we call and pass along a message conveying our "verification" of the veracity of what we type, sign, and mail.

The bureaucrat sending the message includes her e-mail address with her message, tempting me to send a reply to the insecurity. It is an irresistible temptation for me.

I send a long message in reply, beginning with written confirmation of the clearly authentic typed, signed, and mailed instructions.

I cover as much territory as I can, from my critique of the insecurity age illustrated by the message "code", (We are now all spies and criminal suspects?); to the growing handwriting illiteracy of new generations of schooled children, (A new Rosetta Stone expertise is born: literacy specialists?); to the thoughtlessness or marketing con game of complete stranger government/corporate bureaucrats who automatically use correspondents' first names without first asking consent.

To the non-consensual first name familiarity, I respond by referring to the bureaucrat as our new "best friend" in her organization.

After completing and refining the message wording, I realize that I should convert it into the computer version of handwriting font to emphasize the literacy and familiarity points. So I do.

Mariko laughs when I describe the writing. Unfortunately, I don't have a copy because I reply using the organization's own "secret" system instead of our regular e-mail address.

Mariko and I wonder if the reader will laugh or puzzle blankly over my writing.

In the writing, I tell the bureaucrat reader that she is reading an example of thoughtful correspondence between people who are sufficiently intimately acquainted to be on a first name basis.

Then I change the currently-used "Hello" salutation to "Our dear" followed by the bureaucrat's first name and sign the message with the archaically formal "Faithfully yours".

This is handwritten contemptuous familiarity? Impudent! Someone always has to point out that Emperor Insecurity has no clothes?!

Predictably: The answer is no reply. An answer would be alien. In bureaucracy, no one can hear you laugh.

Besides, no one in bureaucracy is listening and no one in bureaucracy wants to hear you or your laughter.

Just shut up and fill in the form. It's almost like being a lifelong elementary school pupil.

### Not so unknown

There is so much that we don't know about John Doe, but his siblings Joe, Ken, Ju, Iai, Aiki, and Sho are famous.

# Tone deaf & arithmic

Algorithms are not melodious. They're not harmonious with humanity. They're out of tune with real life.

A certain, unnamed company that I try to communicate with has problems with its algorithm, a not uncommon problem with corporate/government bureaucracy.

When the algorithm sees the words "diary" and "review" in my book titles it assumes too little.

It assumes <u>Terrian Journals</u> books are comprised of only blank diary pages because they are "a diary of thoughts in adventure".

It assumes that <u>Terrrian Journals' Exploration of Inner & Outer Space (a review of future writings past)</u> is a critic or book review of some already published book by some other author.

Duh! In my letters correcting these inhuman, non-human errors, I compare the algorithm with a second language learner who Mariko encounters at her dojo.

When Mariko uses the word "degree", the learner insists that it applies only to temperature, nothing else.

Yet when I'm hot in summer, I still have only four degrees, and when I'm cold in winter, I still have an apparently balmy four degrees too.

The language learner must be puzzled when she hears that someone is getting the third degree if it's not winter. It's a rare meteorological phenomenon?

# Retirement planning

Some people say that they have no plans to retire.

Others die of employment, and of other imposed or deliberately acquired burdens, long before they can think about planning to retire.

Is this socio-institutionalized insomnia and torture induced sleep deprivation?

I don't have those life-leaching and premature life-ending problems.

I also have no retirement plans either.

For me, retirement is just a natural human animal state of being, unlike employment and other socio-institutionalization and rote memory blind repetition.

This is how retirement happens:

When I'm tired I yawn, arrange my bed or futons, shower, floss, put on appropriate sleepwear, lie down, close my eyes, and fall asleep.

There is absolutely no retirement planning involved in this almost automatic, nightly behaviour. Those who believe otherwise must be highly-paid "retirement advisors".

The basic message of such "advisors" is essentially always the same. They say stock up on money and things. Then get old and die. Why would anyone pay for such advice?

Maybe it's part of the advisor's own retirement planning.

Are people who pay "retirement advisors" sleep walking? Or are they losing sleep by worrying about retirement planning?

Worrying about retirement planning is an endless and recurring wide-awake nightmare.

Everything in a full life changes all the time, making the long-term, "secure" retirement planning project an almost endless, ongoing process.

It only ends with the death of the always worried person.

If s/he worries enough, s/he will never retire. S/he will probably die of worry before reaching "retirement age". Problem solved?

So there is no point in trying to make a retirement plan and there is no point in paying an "advisor".

This leaves one very significant question unanswered. When does the "retirement age" begin?

Is it when some people decide to be employers and redefine everyone else as employeed, i.e. the new serfs?

It seems doubtful that employers ever truly see retirement as a viable alternative to death.

For employers, dead employeed are preferable to people collecting pensions for many years and doing whatever they please or whatever their aging, declining selves can still do, instead of serving employers, right?

# Play time

I notice the obvious. When I listen to news or music while preparing something or doing other things, it takes me longer to complete them.

So it's surprising that I only now realize that that's why employeed people getting paid by the length of time it takes to finish a job play radios and music while they work.

Employers never figure out this scheme?

Obviously they don't, particularly in restaurants and shops where recorded music and advertising messages are always being played.

When a radio broadcast is turned on in a shop, it may also include commercials for other shops, competitors. This seems to be a strangely unanticipated outcome.

I hear just such commercials in stores in Canada.

Some employers may believe that background sound makes customers remain and return.

Some employers may believe that background sound disorients and confuses customers to the point that they make fewer rational decisions; they are less likely not to make purchases; and/or their impulse shopping urges take over.

All of the above increases the length of time that a customer must stay in a commercial enterprise and thus increase the likelihood of making more purchases?

I find that not having any choice in what's invading my ears makes me more likely to either put plugs in my ears or leave the store as quickly as possible to end the annoyance.

In one Fukuoka store, with a practice of repeating corporate jingles and slogans endlessly, at very loud volume, I stand in front of the "security" camera, gesture that the background sound it too noisy, and make the exaggerated gesture of putting plugs into my ears.

My mime protest actually works. It's a resounding success for a silent act.

In my subsequent visits to the same shop, I find the volume and frequency of playing store advertising decreases dramatically. Consumer action prevails!

Perhaps the shop's money-hungry employers realize that their use of background sound has negative consequences.

The use of background sound is actually accomplishing the opposite of their maximizing-profits business plan.

Employers are jeopardizing their business profits by using background sounds that annoy and drive away customers.

The sound also reduces employeed productivity, just as news and music always slow me down.

When the employeed are slowed down, disoriented, rendered nervous, and annoyed by background sounds, they are less likely to work at full capacity.

They are less capable of serving customers well.

The employed in such unsound, noisy establishments are also more likely to make mistakes, which can become costly for the employer.

So background sound results in a decline in sales, productivity, and profits.

Everyone: Turn off your sounds.

## No memory required

Moneyed people don't need memories to find their cars in parking spots and they also don't need to trust their luxury vehicles to valets.

Moneyed people have chauffeurs.

It's a mute point perhaps, because moneyed people have no memory of humanity or their membership therein.

Humanity is the moneyed person's unknown "outside world".

For the rest of us, car makers make a lucrative attempt to help vehicle owners to neutralize memory loss in parking lots.

The companies do so and increase profits simultaneously. They sell a new product that adds to the vehicle owner's monthly vehicle debt payments.

The new product enables people to use a key chain to send out a radio signal causing horns to honk, lights to flash, and engines to start, telling drivers where to find their vehicles.

But when many vehicle owners entering a parking lot are pushing their key chain buttons at about the same time, each driver doesn't know exactly which horn, lights, and engine belong to his/her vehicle.

The only solution is to wait until the shopping centre closes for the night and walk toward the last vehicles parked in the lot, hoping it doesn't belong to one of the stores' employeed.

But maybe she'll give you a ride home and you can file a missing vehicle report at the police station?

The next move by vehicle manufacturers is a step toward socio-economic equality?  Not quite.  It's toward memory parity with the moneyed.

The next step in resolving the problem of remembering where you park is to introduce yet another new, profit-making product.

Vehicle tracking devices and "smart phone apps" are designed to eliminate the need for the troublesome use of memory and the inconvenient pushing of a button on a key chain to find a vehicle.

These "highly-advanced technologies" fit very well into a Sisyphus standard issue existence (s.i.e.) world and in a time when vehicles can not only drive themselves but also track and locate their former driver rendered docile passenger.

Former vehicle operators no longer have any need for memory.  They're just like moneyed people, right?

To built upon the old saying, some people have "more money than brains", I now add that some people have more technology than brains.

### Building narrative

A one-story building is uneventful. A 50-story building is more promising in the sense of interesting.

This humour makes no sense to me because I insist on using the "archaic" spelling to describe buildings.

### Wa-wa-waaa

My almost total ignorance of medical science and human anatomy tells me that the funny bone sounds as if it extends from the shoulder to the elbow.

I also wonder if all magicians have trick knees.

Do people who regularly walk in the rain end up with cricks in their necks?

And of course someone who plays music recorded on vinyl or shiny plastic at a social event can suffer from a slipped disc.

### Ups & downs

The above heading should not be confused with the apparent source of a common old upset stomach remedy.

The topic of discussion here is a matter of present and past vision. It's a seesaw question.

There are so many words that are ending, or should I say cut off by the past tense.

### Great giveaway

Winnipeg news and cousin Kaeren tell me that households in this city have an annual giveaway day.

It's so popular that homeowners put out signs, and lock up things that they want to keep, to prevent passersby from taking away everything they see sitting around outdoors.

### Old jokes revisited

When U.S. entertainment writers and actors go on strike for the first time in many years, their movie and television show production comes to a halt.

Some previously completed work is still being released, but the comedy that Mariko and I watch disappears.

I dig into the internet archives to find some old situation comedy episodes of 50 years ago, ones by the straight-faced former accountant, Bob Newhart.

It's almost literally gut-splitting humour in my family.

My dad has a hernia operation and I make sure that he does nothing to break the stitches.

The only flaw in my plan is Newhart's show. Seeing the show while recovering from the operation, my dad breaks into uncontrollable, belly-jiggling laughter.

We don't find out the consequences until a few years later, when our family doctor tells my dad that he needs another hernia operation because the previous repair was damaged "soon after that operation".

Yes, during The Bob Newhart Show.

Mariko is familiar with Newhart's more recent work, such as his key role in the hilarious movie "Elf", and his guest star appearances in a very funny television show, "Big Bang Theory".

But The Bob Newhart show is new to Mariko I don't remember or don't previously see many episodes due to my university studies.

I only recall one scene and some guest stars.

So the old comedy is essentially new to us both. It makes us laugh while teaching us something about that fairly recent past society and its ordinary situations.

It shows how a sense of humour changes and the humorous becomes surprising and questionable over time.

This includes making fun of men and women for behaving "normally", i.e. fulfilling stereotypical behaviours that are widely accepted conventions that are imposed on both sexes.

Here's an example of a joke that my dad tells at the time, with the sexism removed.

Two people are riding together in a horse and buggy. The horse stops suddenly.

The person holding the reigns gets off the wagon, walks in front of the horse and says, "That's one." He returns to his seat and the horse moves along.

The same thing happens two more times. The third time the person with the reigns shoots the horse. The passenger is understandably shocked and appalled by the cruelty.

The passenger is very upset with the person holding the reigns. In response, that person says, "That's one."

I make the mistake of telling the joke with the sexism included to a feminist friend. I do so in complete innocence, not to offend or annoy my friend.

She is very annoyed and condemns the joke. I don't understand why the sexist element is more important than the humour itself.

Years later, I realize that the joke is not good in its sexist form because it seems to support and legitimize male control, domination, and abuse of females' lives.

That's because, in the original sexist joke the person holding the reigns is male and the passenger is female.

Of course the joke remains obnoxious for non-sexist reasons too.

It is a joke at the expense of a horse.

Sadly, women are still the butt of jokes when the old TV show is on the air.

Making fun of women for behaving passively, aggressively, and stereotypically is fair game for comedy.

Likewise, male-female relationships. That humour continues even today in every joke about "my girlfriend", "my boyfriend", and my "spouse".

The old TV show is transitional comedy from sexist to less sexist times and illustrates changes in popular addictions.

In this comedic tale of the personal and professional encounters of a psychologist, male insecurity is also revealed.

The characters define "a man" as someone who watches sports on television when not going to games. "A man" also never uses a red "woman's umbrella".

In an age where both "straight" and "gay" males wear bright colours and have many more interests than the sedentary habit of watching sports, "a man" is funny.

Yet the psychologist in this story wears colourful shirts, not just white ones, as is the style beginning in the era of the show.

Only the male airline navigator seems to be somewhat immune from the show's narrow stereotypes. In the show he is often leaving and arriving in an airline uniform.

He can only display his employment identity while struggling to express himself.

It's interesting that at least some episodes of the old show are the product of a female teleplay writer.

Perhaps that's why women are portrayed as very slowly awakening from their stereotypical behaviours of passively accepting what the men dish out until responding angrily in frustration with the male-imposed limitations.

But earlier actors, including Katherine Hepburn and Lucille Ball, do some good experimental and pioneering parts as stronger, more independent female characters.

The women in the Bob Newhart show are starting to become aware of the fact that they want to do more in life than the only available jobs that men restrict them to doing.

As for changing addictions, The Bob Newhart show is remarkable for the prevalence of alcohol drug use for all occasions, even the most casual drop-in of a friend.

Alcohol is portrayed as an enjoyable escape from reality, just like other drugs. Drug consumption and aftereffects are the stuff for more humour.

Drunks and their antics are big jokes that get lots of laughs for singer Dean Martin and Laugh-In comedians. Alcohol overdosing is so funny.

Drunks and alcoholics are the butt of humour and exist to amuse other people. Getting someone drunk is hilarious. "Have another drink. One or two more won't hurt you."

Harmful and abusive behaviours and harmful health effects of the alcohol drug are ignored, sloughed over, or denied during the era of the old TV show.

The slightest mention of these effects still gets the same treatment by the narrowest, most defensive, and most aggressive alcohol users today.

Drunk drivers killing people and causing grief and suffering to survivors are "just bad people". It has nothing to do with alcohol itself. Sure, just like guns in the U.S.

The last laugh comes from the big alcohol companies, lobbyists, other pushers, and the authors of their advertising campaigns. They laugh all the way to the bank.

The consequences of using their product are collateral damage.

But eventually, the alcohol prevalence jokes are no longer funny.

So in today's humour and drama, characters just sit around enjoying each other's company, always with an alcoholic drink in their hands and mouths.

The message remains the same: no alcohol; no fun.

Yes, the alcohol is in softer drug form now, such as "light" beer, instead of the previous "hard liquor" standards of old TV shows and movies.

But at least two other drugs are becoming more prevalent in humour and drama. They are marijuana and cocaine.

Movies starring Cheek and Chong are no longer extra-ordinarily exceptional.

A repertoire movie theatre showing "The Rocky Horror Picture Show" is no longer the only place to do the "soft" drug of choice in the midst of a big audience.

"Crocodile Dundee" is no longer surprised by the presence of powdered drug sniffing at a big city party.

themselves; and who never challenge their own beliefs or the objects of their adoration. They can't <u>take</u> a joke.

Instead, they blindly and fundamentally devote themselves, and in some extreme cases their entire lives, to things not worthy of their undivided attention, reverence, and loyalty.

Humour is serious business and needs to be taken seriously by anyone who believes it's just a tool for attacking other people for being just as bad as the person cracking jokes.

### "Racist" joke's on me

Some humour is about misunderstanding and misinterpreting. This makes harmless puns and other semantic humour possible.

But some joking isn't so innocent or harmless because it implies or overtly states that mocking people who are in some way different from "us" is fair and legitimate.

It's okay for "us" to target "them" because "they're" not "us". "Our" jokes can be critical of "them" because "they" deserve it for not being "us" and not trying to be "us".

Too many "first" world tourists are notorious for this type of humour, making all "third" worlders the butt of jokes.

Some "first" worlders quote from stereotypical joke books written just for them.

One of my least pleasant cousins, after years of living in splendid isolation under the wings of isolated elite parents, laughs badheartedly about one "third" world postal delivery service, quoting from just such a joke book.

The joke states, in part, that the letter carriers "in that place" don't pay much attention to the delivery address or the person who is supposed to receive any item of mail.

So mail can be delivered to the wrong place and person, or just dumped in the garbage.

The punch line is that if the mail is important, the sender will try again or find some other means of transmitting the information in the letter.

My cousin, who never lives in the "third" world nation-state in question, and who only visits there for a few days during a renowned festival, while her husband is selling arms to the then military dictatorship, reads many of the "first" world "joke book" jibes about "that place" out loud.

Then she bursts into hysterical laughter and loudly proclaims to me, when I have yet to explore the nation-state being ridiculed, "It's so true! Isn't it!"

A joke between two ignorant people is only a joke on the two ignorant people.

Ill-humoured, unjustified, and nasty mockery follows in the footsteps of European colonial dictatorship rules, as described in E.M. Forester's A Passage To India.

In that story, when a local person notices that a member of the ruling colonial elite forgets some item of jewellery and lends his identical item to the ruler, it becomes an excuse for faulty humour.

Other members of the ruling colonial elite, who spot the missing jewellery on the local person, are quick to make fun of the thoughtful and generous local person.

They describe the thoughtful, generous person as a typical example of the laughably sloppy local people.

This type of unmerited mockery extends to "joke" books about "Newfies", "Québecois", and anyone else not enjoying "our" ignorant prejudices.

In truth, the ignorant mockers are people who don't understand, don't try to understand, and, at heart, don't want to understand.

The ignorant mockers imagine that "we" are the "superior" "majority", "hardest-working", and "rightful and just rulers of the world"; "we" are the speakers of "the world language", and the benevolent emissaries of "the global culture".

This perspective of "us" and "them" becomes an irony in the lyrics of a much-celebrated and ostensibly beautiful and well-intentioned song composed to help starving children: "We are the world."

Unfortunately, the song reduces feeding children to a non-commital commercial act.

By merely purchasing a record and listening to it "we" save children's lives, until the next mega-famines.

There's no need for any personal commitment, responsibility, sustainable assistance, and substantial thinking. No action is required beyond purchasing a record.

"We" save the world by merely spending money.

So we buy the rights, in perpetuity, to say anything that we want to say about "them" in "our" jokes?

In this light, I almost hesitate to report a personal blunder of misunderstanding in <u>Terrian Journals' Iwitfulness</u> because it's difficult to tell this tale without using harmful and malicious humour in the process of story-telling.

I don't mind recounting the fact that I made a mistake and am deservedly embarrassed publicly for my error. My humour books devote some space to mocking myself.

The best way to re-tell this particular incident is to use the original words that I write at the time. It happens in a small town restaurant in Alaska (U.S.)

After our ride with Pat this morning, she invites us to a rare pancake-with-everything brunch in a cowboy-style restaurant.

We don't miss our camp diet of sandwiches and canned food.

The locals are friendly in the western motif eatery, and as we eat I overhear a couple of them at a neighbouring table talking about hunting. I don't like what I'm hearing.

The vocabulary they use leads me to believe they are racists of European origin who are murdering other locals of African origin.

I can't help but give them a shocked look of disbelief. They know what I'm thinking. They also know that I'm wrong.

They humorously explain that they're using a word that sounds racist only to the ears of someone who has no idea of what they're talking about.

They are using an ordinary word which accurately describes the non-human animal that they're hunting.

The most likely people to take offence at their ostensibly-innocent hunting story are probably vegetarians or animal rights advocates.

But at this point in time, in this restaurant, I am neither.

The racism that I believe I'm overhearing is all in my mind, not in their words. We share a laugh together as they make that fact plain to me.

I'm laughing at myself. They're more than justified in joining me in this hearty and well-deserved self-criticism.

There isn't a racist "under every bed", hiding with the "communists" and "terrorists"?

### Lions share?

Do lions roar with laughter while they're eating up the works of comedians?

### Wave

In Fukuoka and Miyazaki, when an adolescent says, "Haro!" to me I can reply, "Haro chuiho! Kaze sugoi desu ne."

One day while passing between children playing half a block apart, the one in front of me says, to his playmate, "Gaikokugin!"

I respond as if he's talking to me. I turn around and say, "Doko?"

### Exotically funny

Males drool over exotic female dancers in darkened entertainment centres.

But when I wiggle in imitation, my partner Mariko laughs.

After I show our friend Meg how to wink and wiggle her shoulder to attract her boyfriend's attention, and she tries this approach, the results are surprising.

Her boyfriend asks her if she has a stiff shoulder.

### Humour checkers

This isn't a game. It's Mariko and Miyuki. Both are clever and exigent in giving up laughter. Not funny, no laugh.

So if I'm trying to be funny and if what I say breaks them up, I know that I can write it up.

But if only I laugh, I sometimes ignore them and write it up anyway. Humorous licence?

### Break

It can be a fall or a dance. But it can't be a fall dance?

"Give me a break." isn't a request for injury or humour, but it is the equivalent of asking if something is intended to be funny.

A joke can break me up, but a couple doesn't laugh when they follow suit.

Right in the middle of a number of movies, at least a couple of characters will have a break to inhale one of their drugs of choice, just like the old TV show's alcohol habit.

But the new drug culture in humour remains much less pervasive than alcohol was in the past.

At the same time, although drug use remains part of humour, it doesn't go to extremes.

Otherwise popular humour would now be featuring the pain killers, anti-depressants, and weight loss drugs.

Despite the latent sexism and unstated but normalcy-by-example use of the alcohol drug in "The Bob Newhart Show", it is only one illustration of its times, not an exceptional case.

What makes the old TV show particularly good are the combinations of encounters among spouses, co-workers, and patients.

They provide many opportunities for comedy and laughter. The psychologist has as many problems as all of the above, making the interactions become particularly funny.

Bob Newhart's stand-up comedy and character acting are always soft spoken. He understates and provides surprising descriptions of and reactions to everything, ordinary or not.

I am thus inspired to write by merely watching some very old reruns of a TV comedy show.

# Sense of empathy

Humour changes with increased consciousness, empathy, and sincere understanding of the implications of mocking others due entirely to stereotypes or drug addiction.

To dismiss this all as being "politically correct" humour means denying that people and societies change and evolve over time.

Decrying empathy as "politically correct" also means that instead of respecting other people when we joke, we prefer to demean others, to ignore the impacts of what we say and do to others, and to deny that we all need to treat each other better and equally.

Some humour demonstrating the extreme opposite of empathy misrepresents and distorts other people while demeaning, condemning, and demonizing them.

This reminds me of Nazi posters that mock Jewish religionists. Some thoughtless non-Nazis also fall into this trap when they maliciously mock other people.

As mentioned earlier, both a Scandinavian and a French publication seem to confuse the idea of hurting other people with "freedom of speech".

A Nazi would agree with and support this perspective, when authoring diatribes and making "final solution" plans.

Mocking and degrading people for simply being alive and having sacrosanct beliefs is not always funny.

There seem to be so many religionists of all varieties who don't see themselves with clarity; who don't reflect upon

A two-way radio signal has a similarly humourless outcome when it follows suit.

Can't you take a break?

## Feedback

I grow up hearing feedback.  It happens when a loud speaker is inadvertently located too close to a microphone. The speaker should speak more softly?

Now, when government corporate/bureaucracy asks for "feedback", they treat it too as a loud, inadvertent noise that needs to be silenced by distancing speakers from microphones.

Bureaucracy considers feedback a problem requiring silencing instead of requiring actual problem-solving efforts.

## Nonsense syllables

Mispronouncing one language in another can be comical, especially if a speaker of the other language doesn't know what s/he's saying.

One year I send Kumamoto friend Eriko a seasonal greeting with a message that I write in hiragana to convey the type of words normally expressed only in katakana.

Eriko is puzzled when we talk on the phone later, asking me for an explanation.

I ask her to read out loud what I write.  She does, but she has no idea what she's reading.  Each time that she completes a reading, Mariko and I burst into laughter.

Literally, Eriko is saying HABAGOODASAMMA.

Ah! Do I really have to explain this joke?

## CASS

Our friends Collette and Alistaire, who live in Newfoundland & Labrador for many years, work there, and bring up their children.

But due to their birth outside the province, they are forever "from away".

Mariko and I share some hilarity with them, particularly Alistaire. We mirror and reflect our often equally madcap senses of humour.

To clarify, neither of us usually wears any type of hat.

Alistair is a professor with a Doctorate and I am not. What does that say about him and me?

During one of our encounters, I become obsessed with the obsessive use of the word syndrome used by non-medical people to label every perceived sign of an ailment.

So I talk to Collette and Alistaire about made up maladies, such as Alistaire's RITMS, run in the morning syndrome.

Collette, I decide, has AMMQS, ask me many questions syndrome.

For every incident, word, and activity there is a syndrome to name to make up.

Later, in e-mail correspondence, I drive Collette a little bit crazy by making reference to something she mentions as an indication of a syndrome. She has to decipher my letters.

She needs alphabetic radar?

The exchange of letters representing syndromes becomes like deciphering military and other bureaucratic gibberish code words made up to confuse and baffle taxpayers so they won't know what they're paying for and become to intimidated to ask and appear ignorant.

It's CPWMBGS.

## Out and out defective

I understand conventions, norms, religionisms, and cultures as degrees and types of repetitive routines that are passed from one generation to another, like defective inherited genes containing diseases, and that surprisingly go uncured, untreated, and unquestioned for inordinately long periods of time.

This phenomenon shouldn't be confused with personal identity, (endless variations of pan-human "culture"), which, in its most elaborate and advanced form, is the essence of each of us and all of us.

Personal identity is a sense of individual and species uniqueness, not to be confused with egoism, incompatibility, or superiority, i.e. not nationalism.

At best, personal identity shows itself in differences between generations, their attitudes and behaviours, regardless of and often in defiance of defective behavioural genes.

Unfortunately, unquestioned behavioural genes plague all humanity for aeons and show no signs of disappearing. Even the "rebellious" can succumb to them.

Consequently, we're always slipping along a muddy road, sliding off course, and all too often getting stuck in the deep ruts.

It's tragedy and comedy combined.

For me, defective behavioural genes are a source of thoughtful consideration, merited harsh criticism, and humour.

They're easy targets that beg to be hit with rationality, reason, and jokes. So let the jesting continue!

Someone working for the same organization as my parents shows a lack of empathy when he refers to his son's girlfriend.

Evidently, he does so because he's incurably infected with the effects of defective behavioural genes.

He therefore can't psychologically cope with the natural human relationship between his son and his son's girlfriend.

His son and son's girlfriend live together, but their defacto partnership isn't formal, legally licensed, or sanctioned by any government legal paperwork or elaborate religionist ceremony. It's counter-bureaucratic.

So, in terms of defective behavioural genes, the partnership isn't real or legitimate.

This results in the ostensibly funny, but negative way in which the girlfriend is introduced by her partner's father.

He refers to her in social gatherings as his "daughter-in-common-law".

Common law is supported by precedents in court and is integrated into legal statutes and government policies and programmes.

Common law marriage is essentially the equivalent of and a widely accepted alternative to the formal marriage demanded by minds contaminated by defective behavioural genes.

The girlfriend is thus, in actual fact, simply a daughter-in-law. To call her otherwise is intended as a slight that suggests she and her partner are behaving unacceptably.

The only way to become acceptable is to formally marry beyond common law.

It also makes me think about semantics, specifically the term "in-law", i.e. the family of the marriage partner.

In the daughter-in-law case, does her partner's father consider her not to be a real in-law?

So she's an outlaw? And her partner is also an outlaw in the eyes of her family?

So all married couples who aren't conventionally married, according to defective behavioural genes, are outlaws and so are their respective families?

Anyone operating and functioning outside the dictates of defective behavioural genes, even if not breaking or violating any legal statute or precedent, is by definition an outlaw?

So all of my thoughts and writings are outlaw prose?

That's outlawdish! It's a new word I'm coining here and now. I don't expect it will ever be used by anyone anywhere again.

This new word shouldn't be confused with culinary items such as outlandish, or as the U.K.ers say, "outlawndish". Add a mixed beverage and this can become a punch line.

### H0 HO HO H$_2$O

Lack of water is called dehydration. The opposite is hydration. So what is carbohydration? It must be sugar and water? Or is it drinking pop?

### Metamorphosis

Any water vessel, except a glass, mug, or cup, can be amphibious if it's being toad.

### Pisces

Eat fish before sleeping in Brooklyn, New York City, and wake up oily.

### Incorrect weekend

Sinophones and Japanophones are described as people who have difficulty pronouncing "r" and "l", but they aren't the only ones with that problem.

In such cases, when a weekend break is extended by one day, they're apt to say it's a wrong weekend?

Some anglophones, particularly ones from the England area of the U.K. (U.Q.?", have the same difficulty with "r" when they say words such as "ratha" and "weatha".

No wonder anglophones have difficulty learning how to pronounce strong Rs in español and en français.

Yet some of the anglophones I meet continue to talk about people from other language groups having difficulty pronouncing words containing letters such as L, R, B, and V.

So forget about how about anglophones mangle Japanese words?  It's okay because the manglers are anglophones?

### Pseudo-Canuck

A growing number of Canadians speak at least two languages, including at least one of Canada's official languages.

So a Canadian unilingual anglophone can now be defined.

It's someone who can't tell the difference between her/himself and a U.S.er.  Or it's someone who believes the only difference is monarchy.

In some cases, a unilingual francophone might be defined as someone who believes s/he isn't living in Canada.

Of course that would exclude all of the Québec francophone politicians who speak English, such as all the leaders of the separatist political parties in Québec.

## Pole results

The latest poles suggest that there are babies being born in Poland; dogs have an endless supply of urine; and the wireless age has utility lines hanging in the air.

Gallop poles are equestrian?

Conducting a pole must be either exclusive to orchestras in the eastern part of Europe or something to do with make-shift string instruments.

Running a pole is probably some sort of exhibition of logging skills performed on water or high in the air.

Commissioning a pole is a military promotion?  So a pole can be decommissioned too?

Pole land is obsessed with poles.

## Savoury Sverige

Our Sverige friends Jan and Eva introduce us to local delicacies including rice porridge.  But when we're going beyond their home near Lund, we find other dishes.

This is challenging.

Although Scandinavia is less expensive than the U.K. and offers much better quality food, we have to make sure that our limited budget always brings us nutritious food.

This includes whole grain bread, fruit, and vegetables.

Since we are more often on the move than able to store and prepare meals when we are between setting up residences, we need portable food that we can just eat and finish.

In some lands we buy tins of food, but bad chemicals lining tins and "security" rules obliging us not to carry a simple pen knife can opener make our eating more challenging.

So in Scandinavia we start buying smaller bags of frozen vegetables. We thaw and eat them using free hot water in sturdy paper cups. They're for tea.

I start calling our instant healthy meal of frozen vegetables in a land known for cold winters "Sverige food".

### Sting operation

If someone is distinguished it simply means that it is possible to tell him/her from others.

If this isn't possible or becomes impossible, is s/he extinguished?

Bees, wasps, hornets, etc. are surgeons?

### Fashioned after

Every type of clothing has an official or unofficial name or designation.

Coats are named for meteorological phenomena. There are fog coats and rain coats. Reign and rein coats are for horses?

Trench coats aren't always spy wear and are perhaps originally part of an ensemble with trench mouth. If worn in a sloppy manner, they are malwear.

There's a double sexist origin for dish wear, associated with dinner wear, i.e. food spills? Why are there no breakfast or lunch wears?

Soft wear is obviously silk, no pun intended. Hard wear is too small, too big, or unattractive. Mal wear is a poor fit or inappropriate for any occasion.

Underwear may not be a favourite or seldom used. Clothing worn too frequently should be called overwear.

Silver wear is less expensive jewellery. Wear and tear are disposable clothing.

Wear out isn't for indoors.

Outwear indicates that no further invitations will be available until the person changes clothing.

Western wear has no equivalent in other compass points. It can't be worn there either.

Weary or wary is the clothing worn by a clothed person. Beware is black and yellow or orange.

## Message

A message for people who like crosswords:

Try to be nice.

**Acting up**

Western theatre requires a stage coach behind the team.

## Quasi-amphibious inflation

Universities raise admission standards, obliging secondary schools to redefine 70% results as 90% results. The students admitted remain the same calibre.

University students pay ten times my annual tuition for half a year, but don't obtain an education twenty times better than mine.

University administration bureaucrats aren't twenty times more efficient and professors aren't twenty times better than the ones I encounter.

At a university, no one is called a knower. Academic staff with seniority are only called professors. They only profess to know or provide an "educated guess" in guarded words.

Universities continue to offer degrees of education which aren't measures of either warmth or cool comfort. There is no real comfort zone beyond graduation.

"Post-doctoral" studies are make work projects for registrars' offices and other academic bureaucrats.

Those "advanced" studies remind me of Québec's CEGEP system of delaying departure. It doesn't prevent young students' flight to neighbouring provinces.

Professional students, not to be confused with lifelong learners, are like repeat offenders seeking re-incarceration within the familiar walls and corridors of apparent stability and reliable routines provided by institutionalization.

S.I.E. Sisyphus is not restricted to any age, sex, occupation, or educational background.

Government/corporate bureaucracy shows its appreciation for the latest crop of new university graduates by asking them if they know how to type.

Further appreciation of a university education is shown by giving preference to graduates who have more than a degree. They require a community college certificate too.

Never to be completely outsmarted and outwitted, community colleges rebrand themselves "university college" in some political jurisdictions.

That's how to confuse everyone, including the "university college" instructors who I know.

Another approach at inventive nomenclature is renaming a polytechnical institute a university. This increases the number of university grads with non-university credentials.

Having taken a couple of polytechnical courses out of curiosity and interest, I now find that I actually have an academic record with more university courses listed on it.

Government/corporate bureaucracy's oldest trick to erode the confidence of university grad job applicants, and to demean all of them, with or without university degrees, is to demand work experience.

Before the question is posed, the obvious answer, for both the youngest applicants and the employers is - "I have no work experience."

The employer can then follow through on its premeditated plan to pounce upon the young applicant for employment.

The employer seizes the upper hand gained by the "work experience" question and sends the "successful" applicant to the depths of under-employment, there to pursue only meaningless bland chores for the sole purpose of "proving" her/himself worthy of the employer.

The irony of it all is that the "work experience" thus gained is, in itself, of little or no value to the employer. It is merely a waste of a "human resource" to instill obedience.

A disappointed suitor deceived by a non-reciprocated, unappreciated, or unrequited admiration or adoration of another person will more than likely at least provide that person with glowing compliments and a shower of gifts?

The employer's abusive behaviour only moulds a mercenary attitude and only gains obedience, often grudging, that is never earned and never adequately rewarded.

Yet employers all too often embrace the military boot camp like degradation and humiliation of younger employment applicants, as if it were a very useful and effective tool.

Employers seem to believe that the tool is very useful for persuading hardworking and intelligent but under-confident younger people, and intelligent, studious younger people that their very existence, learning, and knowledge are of no value and they lack the "merit" required for employment.

It is common knowledge that, in many cases, "work experience" can only mean after school and summer jobs, including construction labour work, supermarket stock shelving, newspaper route delivery, etc.

This type of work experience is most likely to prepare a younger person for the lifelong pursuit of s.i.e. Sisyphus instead of a fulfilling life.

But even this approach to "work experience" is flawed.

When I ask a supermarket manager if I can work at his store, he replies by asking if I have any grocery experience.

This is a joke? No. He tells me to come back when I do.

I should reply that I have much experience eating groceries and since both of my parents are employed, I often become the designated grocery shopper during office hours.

All I reply is "No." and leave the premises wondering what special expertise I would require to put groceries on shelves.

Beyond the grocery domain, my approach to the bureaucracy's "experience" question is to blind side it by only working in summer jobs and only those related to my actual interests and studies.

I have no difficulty finding this work even without "work experience". I find employers who want me to do what interests me. They aren't exceptional in my "experience".

I don't have to audition for what I want to do by doing what I don't want to do, i.e. doing anything for money and an s.i.e. Sisyphus pat on the head.

When a person does what s/he doesn't want to do in order to do what s/he wants to do, it seems like a bad joke that is both contradictory and self-defeating.

I want to work in law enforcement, so I'm going on a crime spree.  I want to be a dentist, so I'm gorging myself on sugar.  I want office work, so I'm paving roads.

Yes, I do find merit in starting as a mail room clerk and doing all the jobs in an organization as an essential qualification for becoming a CEO or board member.

That way the eventual boss learns everything about the organization; listens to all of the employees met in all of the jobs; almost literally walks in their shoes.

And in the end, the CEO or board member should conclude that s/he has no right to have a superiority complex and that s/he does not merit an income exceeding the salaries of most or all of the other employeed.

Fulfillment isn't measured in money, possessions, titles, or status.  It is measured in the quality of the person and his/her behaviour toward others.

Doing something unappealing as a means of being granted permission to do something appealing is like the grossly inegalitarian exchange of giving an employer almost an entire year of service in order to gain only seven to 30 days of annual vacation.

Other days off are provided by government laws and union agreements, not employers.

Another lopsided part of the deal is to provide the employeed with a monthly pension lower than his/her income, when s/he retires and becomes elderly, but only so long as s/he lives.

Pensions die with the retired.

For most people, pensions aren't endless reparations payments from employers, perpetually contributing to family or community well-being, a legacy from the employer and employeed for the benefit of others.

Pensions also turn out to be a pittance in the context of the lifespans of most people.

The likelihood of someone employed for 20 to 40 years collecting a pension for another 20 to 40 years is not supported by longevity statistics.

Equal retirement years for equal work years is unlikely for most employeed.

So when an employer offers lifelong employment, the most rational and reasonable reply can only be, "You've got to be kidding!".

Employment and s.i.e. Sisyphus are a dirty joke ridiculing billions of people.

### William Otto Oli

Billionaire autocrats and oligarchs encourage the employeed to oppose, denounce, attack, and overthrow all the "elites", except for the billionaire autocrats and oligarchs.

The "elites" are bad, according to billionaire autocrats and oligarchs, because they want to democratize everything for everyone, including the employeed and corporations owned by the billionaire autocrats and oligarchs.

How gauche! (French for left.)  How sinister! (Latin for left.)

## So.

Answering every question the same way is going a long way beyond the mindless and insulting repetition of fixed phrases used for explaining and attempting to justify every manner of restricting and oppressing others and all of us.

Now the answer to every question begins by merely saying, "So."  That's just a simple "So.", not a "So?"  or a "So!".

So, it's the solution to everything?  There's no apparent age limit on the use of this one word answer for all.

So, it's time to say so long after coming so far.  So much for that!  So, it's eternal inflation again.

So, we are living in a world of solitude, playing solitaire solo.  So, yes, very.  So, we can all move to Sochi, use soap and soak.

So, people are suffering from sorghum, also called gingivitis?

So, beginning every response with "So" sounds like, "I'm not interested in what you're saying and I'm not listening to your question.  So here's what I want to say.  Bite me."

So, is this pugilistic Sophism?

So, everyone is becoming a "So" and "So" or a "sob"? How sad and caninely sexist.

The "So." answer makes life much easier for the grandson of our very generous and kind neighbour, Kiomi.

When anyone asks, "What's your name little boy?", he can reply, "So."

That is his actual name.

So, life for every seamstress is also simplified, when anyone asks, "What do you do?" But the retort may turn out to be, "So what?"

So, anglophones can now speak basic Japanese without learning a word of the language and without knowing it.

To the questioning remark in Japanese, "Nice day, isn't it?" the anglophone not knowing s/he's speaking Japanese can always reply, "So."

But whenever I ask a question, I now have to quiver a bit in anticipation, wondering if the person I'm trying to talk with might try to answer my question but won't say so.

It can't be "So"!

Is society becoming more permissive? Everything now automatically gets a say "So".

Poetry and musical compositions find nothing new in the latest all purpose answer word. Sonatas and sonnets are commonplace. SOCAN is prevalent too.

Ships have a long history of using SONAR.

There are now solar power arrays.

Some people frequent solariums. That's a two so sentence.

Timid parents confine their children to soccer.

People in the U.S. drink soda, i.e. pop.

Travellers have sojourns.

Disappointed people can take solace, for maybe not so fast relief.

"So you won't talk, eh!"

"Soylent green is people!"

### Gaining the feed

In Sverige, people eat Swedish food.

In Nippon, people eat seaweedish food.

### Twisted tongues

Some anglophones and francophones tell me that people with their mother tongues are not so good at language learning.

So people from those language groups who do learn other languages well, including me, are strange anomalies?

It's particularly funny (strange) when, in officially bilingual Canada, anglophone politicians and bureaucrats struggle to use French and their francophone counterparts have the same problem with English but...

SRC (Société Radio Canada) reports from the officially unilingual anglophone U.S.A. capital city and interviews U.S. government officials who speak both English and French so well, with impeccable fluency and ease.

Of course the tourist industry, interpreters, and language business establishments are overjoyed by the steady supply of linguistically incompetent paying customers who they gain from the throngs who believe they are "typical" linguistic incompetents.

It's a religionism and a great excuse for not doing well in language tests and for not being able to understand or talk to other people in another language.

"I can't learn another language well because of the nation-state and linguistic group into which I'm born."

This is said with a straight face, as if it were irrefutable gospel truth.

The conclusion is that "we" can never truly understand "them".  So language learning and teaching are futile. Misunderstandings and war are inevitable.

Funny, before learning another language, I experienced great misunderstandings among people who also spoke only one language, my first language.

Ask anyone with a same language boyfriend or girlfriend. "S/he doesn't understand me.  S/he never listens."

In Canadian politics, when dominantly francophone Québec boycotts federal-provincial negotiations during the second coming of Premier Robert Bourrasa, the anglophone premiers fight among themselves in only one language.

Canada never has a "language problem", a favourite pairing of words among master racist unilingual anglophone Canadians who want to assimilate, eliminate, and neutralize all non-anglophones. Take the residential schools, please!

The real problem dividing humanity in Canada is ignorance manifested in isolationism, parochialism, and intranational xenophobia verging on a self denial nihilism.

In the larger world, with 6,000 languages, there is also no "language problem".

Diverse linguistic identities are not a "problem". They are a wealth of interhuman expressiveness.

In the larger world, the problem is nationalism and its mass delusions, illusions, mega-egoism, and bellicose jingoism which reaches the extremes of human self-destruction.

What can be more divisive and dangerous to all human life than a nation-state that solemnly believes and declares that it's the "last best hope for the world"?

This is a deadly serious destructive joke that one particular nation-state is playing on human life today.

It's bizarrely logical and more than subtly implied conclusion is that without this one particular nation-state, i.e. the "last best hope", the world comes to an end.

This could be a hilarious illustration of a superiority complex gone mad if it were not taken so seriously by its absolutist proponents and devout adherents.

They are armed with enough nuclear arms to single-handedly wipe out almost all life on earth.

The "last best hope" indicates that this particular nation state imagines that it is the ultimate pinnacle of human achievement and there is nothing better to look forward to in future.

The true believers in this particular nation-state can only conclude that if the "last best hope" is in peril, then all humanity in the rest of the world becomes expendable, an acceptable loss, and collateral damage to save "our" nation.

Take Vietnam and Afghanistan, please!

All humanity living beyond the "last best hope" must "pay any price and bear any burden" to ensure the survival of only one particular nation-state.

It sounds like a variation of a suicide note left by a very possessive and abusive murder-suicide criminal.

But, getting back to linguistic incompetence, falsely depicting the natural existence of more than one human language as a problem dividing humanity can serve at least two purposes.

One purpose is an attempt to justify forcing people abroad to learn European languages.

Oh, we just need their help, i.e., collaborators for our domineering occupational regimes; unfettered access to their "free" raw materials; and a steady supply of slaves to build our colonial infrastructure, our palaces, our churches, and our agribusiness.

The other most obvious purpose of calling the existence of more than one human languages a problem is that it can serve as a longstanding excuse for horrific genocide and acculturation.

Oh, we didn't understand what we were doing!? Hundreds of years later we will humbly apologize and not discuss compensation or reparations.

You can't right past wrongs, right? We're prepared to let bygones be bygones. Let's just have reconciliation and make it all go away.

But the half-baked theory of "natural" linguistic incompetence lives on and makes successful language learners look ingeniously strange.

When my friend Denis Cantin hears Mariko's ever-improving French and her flawless English, he calls her a genius. Nice compliment accepted.

But my partner Mariko doesn't believe that she's a genius, despite efforts to persuade her that language learning is her very special gift and she is one of the very few who have it.

Mariko attributes her growing array of language skills to fascination with languages and very hard work studying them. She doesn't mean difficult when she says hard.

Resistance to Mariko's version of herself and her language skill development is relentless.

Unable to fathom Mariko's highly successful efforts in language learning, less studious and less fluent people endow her with superpowers and special physiological traits.

She has a "special" tongue and "special" ears that enable her to attain complete fluency and total comprehension. Her response:

To which I can only add:

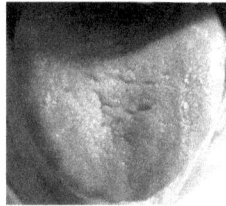

**Incorrigible**

For a while, I'm safe, until Mariko studies French. Up to then, when I make a mistake in English spelling I can claim that I'm confused with the French spelling.

After all, I'm one of the many pupils in primary school who gets to use the "feather pen" for a week after getting a perfect mark on the weekly spelling test in English.

Once that Mariko's knowledge of French grows, she quickly finds out that my claim of confusion with French is not true. My English spelling errors are not French at all.

My next language refuges are Español and Portuguese. Then Mariko studies Español.

Again, she discovers that my English mistakes have no relationship with another language.

Since my Portuguese becomes Porteñol, I'm hard pressed for a refuge now. I have to pay more attention to my English language dictionaries.

Then Mariko begins studying Russian. Unlike me, she never claims that this languages accounts for her mistakes in her other languages.

She can't do that because she doesn't make mistakes in languages.

### The parking lot revolt?

When my parents go on guided tours abroad run by the tourist industry, every time they see a group assembling or signs in a language they can't read, the tour guide says, "Oh. It's a festival."

Thus linguistically disadvantaged "first" world tourists miss out on the protests and revolutions abroad.

To some extent, this explains the "first" worlder "mystery" of why "they" "hate" "us".

If "first" worlders weren't such anglophone and anglophile linguistic isolationists, the world could be a better place for us all.

Unlike anglophone tourists on guided tours of the "outside" world, I'm inclined the other way.

I tend to presume that an assemblage that I don't understand is a political event or the like.

My experience of Direitas Já in Rio; partisan rallies in Córdoba; election night in Mendosa; May Day in Tokyo; a demonstration in Buenos Aires; and the toppling of a dictator in Bangladesh; influence the way I see groups.

So when I see a younger male holding a red kanji placard in front of one of the supermarkets that I frequent in Sawaraku, I ask him if it's a strike.

He explains, but I don't understand. So I ask his permission to take a photo of his sign. He cordially invites me to do so. Later, I ask Mariko to explain it.

She tells me that the sign is asking people who want to sell agricultural products to shoppers at the supermarket not to park in the supermarket parking lot.

Right. What a revolting development this isn't.

### On the wall

The motto over the front door of the building says, "Down For The Count". It's not a training gym for poor boxers. It's the motto of an oral blood donor clinic in Transylvania.

### Farm traffic

Farmland that I know of doesn't have traffic signals or signs, such as speed limits, warnings about road conditions, and stop signs.

But there are yield signs, at least once per year.

### Old joke

Older people tell me that they buy and use PADDs because that's the only way they can communicate with their grandchildren. What a sad lot.

(A PADD is a personal advertising delivery device posing as an essential item in life that one must carry and keep "on" at all times.)

I thought the grandparents' explanation might explain why there seem to be so many older-looking people using PADD. But I could be wrong.

Apparently PADD and other electronic devices emit blue light, which is the artificial source equivalent of Ultraviolet A from sunlight. UV age ages skin.

So the PADD users I'm observing may in fact be 25 year olds who only look as if they are 85.

### Celling out

An older-looking woman, probably younger because she's addicted to PADD, tells me that her friends, who I never meet, find me strange entirely because I have no cell phone.

She therefore concludes that she can't be friends with a person who doesn't have a cell phone. That's me.

She adds, a strange consolation(?), that cell phone ownership is an essential prerequisite for becoming her friend or a friend of her friends, entirely due to the culture into which she and her friends are born.

The "culture" is celled up?

She truly must be a younger person who is looking aged entirely due to PADD UV rays?

But she looks deceptively as if she was born before cell phones, i.e. before her "culture" made owning a cell phone a precondition of being a friend.

### Under litigation?

A famous rock star from Eire probably has trouble finding a lawyer because s/he has to work pro-Bono.

### Ups & downs

People who consider it normal to combine caffeine and nicotine use are quite correct.

Caffeine addicts use their drug for awakening, stimulating, and agitating themselves.

Nicotine addicts use their drug to calm down.

Alcohol addicts use their drug to "reduce inhibitions" and restore a sense of natural human expression, without actually experiencing that expression.

This drug provides only a temporary and artificial illusion, probably to keep the addict sane, by counterbalancing the artificial restrictions imposed upon humans by artificial, stultifying, and oppressive societies, i.e. most societies, if not all.

### Yikes!

People fearing rodents may eek out a living.

### T message

Someone is wearing a T-shirt in Fukuoka's shikatetsu with these words printed on it in this manner:

TECHNO
LOGICAL

The logic escapes me.

But then again, I never find saying the word "that" funny.

### Leave 'em gagging

Although humourless "AI" is trying to alter my keystrokes to enter words that I don't write or intend to write, making me unintentionally funny, despite my great resistance to this daffy AI meddling in **my** writing, this segment of writing isn't the resulting gag reel, out-takes and bloopers collection, or what's left on the cutting room floor.

This segment is about a tendency in broadcast news to divert its efforts away from covering news and towards entertaining its anonymous mass audience.

The best of this type of broadcasting prides itself on at least providing comic relief to end a daily news report devoted to crime, chaos, disruptions, tragedies, and disasters.

It's called "leave 'em laughing".

Unfortunately, some broadcasts now stretch this leaving humour into greetings and interruptions, fillers in the middle of actual news coverage.

This follows a long tradition started by Laugh-In Looks At The News, The Royal Canadian Air Farce, Weekend Update on Saturday Night Live, and This Hour Has 22 Minutes.

"Viral" videos rivalling "funniest home movies" now appear randomly interspersed between actual news stories. News hosts need toilet breaks?

Of course, the least funny part of news broadcasting, causing more laughter, is the unintended humour described elsewhere in <u>Terrian Journals</u> books of humour, i.e. basic language errors by anglophones and anglophiles.

### Ox leaks

What would a series of humour books be without any reference to Canadian political science professor and author, and humour writer Stephen Leacock?

Funny you should ask?

I enjoy his amusing short stories and become curious about his political science writings. I also discover that he writes a couple of books about humour itself.

But sometimes it's better not to get to know an author too well?

His books about humour are, unfortunately, filled with generalizations about "higher humour" belonging to "higher' civilizations".

In my experience, a person's sense of humour depends on the person, not his/her place on the mythical higher "civilization" ladder.

Otherwise I wouldn't be able to find a wide range of people in many different civilizations, socio-economic groups, and nation-states who laugh at my jokes, right?

In his books about humour, Leacock appears to uncritically regurgitate the apparently widely accepted and parroted myths of his times about distinctions among humans made up by nationalists and other racists.

These books reflect the fact that they are written during the time of the rise of Nazis and Fascists in Europe and the continued widespread prevalence of racism in the Americas. These are "higher civilizations?"

The lack of critical thinking about humour is surprising coming from a renowned political science professor who writes the internationally acclaimed English-language text book of his times about political science.

While analyzing history and "civilizations" in his books about humour, Leacock unwittingly fails to emphasize that humour in any time frame is not so easily generalizable.

How many people in their teens now laugh at the mention of "sock it to me"?

But more personally, when it comes to Professor Leacock, the joke is on me and other comparatively novice humour writers.

We pay an entry fee and buy ten copies of our own books to give to a humour writing contest named for the professor.

The contest information literature suggests that the books we give to the contest judges may be donated to public libraries, at the judges' discretion.

Are they going into recycled paper or land fill?

Thinking positively, I guess the judges all like my book so much that they keep it. I find no sign of it when I search public library records across the country.

The entry fee from contestants is apparently to pay for a cash prize for the winning contestant.

Then, at almost the last possible moment, a famous humour writer who makes a fortune producing and starring in an internationally-syndicated comedy television show for years, and who already publishes humour books too, enters the contest.

Guess who wins the prize money provided by novice writers who give away ten copies of their books?

This reminds me of the time that I interview Arnold Edinborough, who is appointed to publicize a contest to name "The New Massey Hall" in Toronto.

Instead of simply naming the hall using that already established name, the committee responsible announces that it wants members of the public to submit suggestions.

A prize will go to the person sending in the name chosen.

Then newspaper magnate Roy Thompson's group, an organization with long pockets that makes generous donations, suggests the new hall be named after him.

The winning entry is thus chosen. It's "Thompson Hall".

What a coincidence!

Last time I checked, the old Massey Hall still existed in Toronto. Who paid for the renovations, Thompson?

### Finale

It's very difficult to finish this book because every time that I think I'm on the last page, something funny happens.

# Tail end tale

Sometimes the surprising is standing right in front of you, going unnoticed until you take a close look. Such is the case when I'm going home from a dental cleaning.

There he is, directing traffic for some "security service". I don't know which one, but the company's name begins with an "a".

Does someone in "security" actually have a sense of humour or is someone making a comment on the current insecurity obsession.

Or this is a "security" breachless?

(This is an unaltered photo with nothing cut off.)

**VOLUMES FROM MYTHBREAKER**

<u>**Terrian Journals series**</u>:
A Sketch of Terrian History
Terrian Journals' How To Make The Nation
Terrian Journals' 500 Years In Louis Bourbon's Few Hectares
Full Employment: Not Fulfilling
Terrian
Caretaker Society
Terrian Journals: Living as a Newcomer
Middle Earth Journals
Rediscovery Journals
Fukurokuju No Kasumi Journals

Sabbatical Journals
Departure Journals
Adventuredate Unknown Journals
Away Team Journals
Searching For South Journals
Inonakanokawazu Journals
КАЗАНЬ Journals
Exile Journals
Tenjin Journals
Next Journals
Terrian Journals for the Misguided
Terrian Journals' N.S.R.: Not Spying, …Really!
TJ JNG:  Terrian Journals' Jokes Nobody Gets
Terrian Journals' Half Serious
Terrian Journals' Iwitfulness
Terrian Journals' Disbelief
Terrian Journals' House Trap
Terrian Journals' Virtually Camping
Terrian Journals' Crystal
Virtually Dead
Terrian Journals' Maximum Insecurity
Terrian Journals' Mandarinas
Terrian Journals First Anthology
Terrian Journals Second Anthology


<u>**Pre-Terrian Journals:**</u>
Explorations Of Inner & Outer Space
Out of Context
Terrian Journals Origins


<u>**Archway series**</u>:
Archway: Six Year Book of Dreams
Archway: Lifetime Rhyme
Archway: Life Before Dreams
Archway's Valentine Love
Archway's Garden Rhymes
Archway's Christmas New Years Rhymes


<u>**Additional Titles**</u>:
Language Learning Secrets
Trying To Teach Languages In The L.B.E. World
An Adult Book About Education
Terrian Journals' Miss Schooling?


<u>**Fiction::**</u> Terrian Journals' Political Science Fiction

www.ingramcontent.com/pod-product-compliance
Lightning Source LLC
LaVergne TN
LVHW051549080426
835510LV00020B/2927